WARRIOR

The Life and Lessons of a Man Who Beat Cancer for 57 Years

A BIOMYTHOGRAPHY NOVEL BY
Brent Green

Brent Green & Associates, Inc.

Denver, Colorado

2018

Also by Brent Green

Noble Chaos: A Novel
Marketing to Leading-Edge Baby Boomers
Generation Reinvention
Questions of the Spirit
Are You Still Listening? Stories & Essays from 1969

Copyright © 2018 by **Brent Green**
All rights reserved

No part of this publication may be reproduced, distributed or transmitted in any form or by any means, without prior written permission. For information about permission to reproduce selections from this book, write to the publisher.

Brent Green & Associates, Inc.
1011 S. Valentia St. Suite #86
Denver, Colorado 80247

Visit the book website: http://www.warriornovel.com

Library of Congress Cataloging-in-Publication Data is available

ISBN-10: 0692366296
ISBN-13: 978-0692366295

Library of Congress Control Number: 20113917214
CreateSpace Independent Publishing Platform
North Charleston, South Carolina

Printed in the United States of America
Book cover design by Twist Design Group, Denver, Colorado

Publisher's Note: This is a work of fiction. Names, characters, places, and incidents are a product of the author's imagination. Locales and public names are sometimes used for atmospheric purposes. Any resemblance to actual living persons or to businesses, companies, institutions, or locales is completely coincidental.

Grateful acknowledgement for historical background provided by: *Achieving Wellness through Risk Taking: The End of Boredom,* © 1985 by Dr. Mark Crooks

This is a novel inspired by the life of G. Mark Crooks, Ph.D. (1945 — 2010), one of the bravest persons I have known. I dedicate this book to him, wishing that his inimitable wellness and survival lessons will reach future generations.

Although influenced by actual events, all incident details, names, and characters in this biomythography are imaginary.

CONTENTS

Acknowledgements 1

Jump 3

Nemesis 17

Lover 27

Crash 43

School 59

Patient 77

Coronary 91

River 107

Breathe 123

Skyscraper 141

Fierce 155

Redemption 167

Afterword 181

ACKNOWLEDGEMENTS

I would like to acknowledge guidance and support given to me by many friends, family members and colleagues, a few of whom I shall mention here.

I wish to thank my parents, Lucille and Gilbert Green, who after sixty-seven years of successful marriage, passed away from natural causes less than twenty-four hours apart. Their concluding days impressed upon me how hospice care can truly usher the dying toward a good death, as each person defines it. Julie Bethke, my late sister who also finished her life with hospice care, shared and guided those profound final days with our parents, and her calmness reassured and strengthened me.

Dr. Ken Cinnamon, my college roommate and Mark's acquaintance, offered much needed advice, critical commentary, and encouragement to help propel this writing journey forward to conclusion. Dr. Donald Vest, my close advisor for over 45 years, consulted with Mark concerning positive risk-taking and with me about the psychology of flow experiences.

Mostly, my thanks to Mark, who became my friend and fitness mentor in 1973 and remained a continuing, positive influence for the next thirty-seven years.

His gentle authority lives on.

Chapter 1

JUMP

June 1980, a bridge in Kansas City, Missouri

I stood on the illegal side of a guardrail near the apex of the Paseo Bridge, the choppy Missouri River nine stories below, distance to impact enough to snap my back and kill me. A scarlet sun lifted from the eastern horizon, defining this moment as beginning or ending. Not far away, an approaching diesel engine growled and grumbled. I was aware of background noises, but I had learned to disengage: an asset to achieving dangerous goals, a liability limiting situational awareness.

Dreading humiliation, I stared at choppy coffee waters, imagining my landing spot: a gulch running through the river's midway point where our scuba-diving surveillance team had found the best location below the bridge, an entry point of minimum depth, free of impaling junk, about ten feet south of a concrete support. I had planned to leap into twenty feet of water, but now the deepest point measured nine feet. A rushing eighteen-wheeler plus river depth equal to the diving end of a swimming pool could conspire to become disaster. Logical analysis waved warning flags, noted and ignored.

I had earned the self-confidence and fitness to balance on a ledge above that shrinking river, intending survival rather than suicide. I dread heights, and this day would become another display of liberation from fear and boredom. Some call it psychosensory restitution—mind over matter. I had planned every detail and anticipated improbable possibilities. Bring on uncertainty. That is life's essential unpredictability, even for desk-bound bureaucrats shackled to their computers. They don't get it, and that was another reason why I would jump for a more engaged existence.

I became a Greek Titan measuring the Aegean Sea far below towering limestone cliffs, feeling raw authority surge through me, seeing sinewy muscles and collar-length hair waving in the wind. This was not a daredevil stunt, mere sensationalism; this was mind, will, and fitness merging into steel resolve, demonstrating the lessons I had often taught college students and professional athletes. This was the same man wearing a white coat who had saved myocardial infarction victims from permanent disabilities and then more heart attacks.

My mistress, the Missouri, took on human qualities, something we sports psychologists call *personification*. She became soft, supple, and sensuous. She became languid and inviting. She beckoned with wide open arms, awaiting a swift and certain plunge into her depths, all nine feet from surface to silt. We would be united, her flowing contours eager to reward my advances.

I wore a black diver's suit that might offer some insulation upon impact, binding my anatomy as the force of concrete-water punched my feet. Manufactured from one-quarter-inch neoprene insulation, the armor was practical under the circumstances, but this actor preferred to wear merely a loincloth as if immune to human fragilities. Practicality had prevailed over fantasy often since I achieved dual doctoral degrees and embraced more deliberate choices of frontier exploration. Learning and daring compete within, an unsettling battle for compromise. The scientist usually surpasses a romanticist.

My goal was to leap from the bridge and will myself into perfect vertical posture, overcoming the human body's tendency to teeter forward due to disproportionate weight of the trunk over the legs. I planned to become an arrow, straight in flight with no wobbles, toes pointed, fingers closed, and hands pressing lateral to my butt so my arms could not then be dislocated upon impact.

If my calculations and preparations had been adequate, supported by six months of obsessive groundwork, I would slide into the water without damage, becoming the first human not to die from that jump location off the infamous Kansas City bridge. Several tortured souls had leaped from there to death, and that's why I had chosen to make this place of gloomy memories my launching pad into the abyss, the stage for a triumphant return. I had planned to succeed at exploding from waters where others had perished, determined to conquer this consecrated suicide location.

But the goddamn truck roared closer.

In peripheral vision, I saw Jamie waving her hand-scribbled sign to warn the trucker: *Slow Down, Jumper Ahead*. This should have compelled an alert driver to downshift or tap his brakes. I tossed off a thought: exhausted from an overnight haul from Chicago and goosed up on NoDoz and coffee, the teamster might not care if another idiot is suicidal. The other side of the bridge would soon appear in his rearview mirrors. No cops. No compromises. Pedal to the metal. Salina or bust.

I had no time for further calculations because our launch window was closing as morning traffic built into rush hour. Cops would soon arrive. I needed to jump right away: a now-or-never dilemma. Risk-taking demands taking risks no matter how well planned. Uncertainty always prevails. At some point, you've got to jump.

Jamie's warnings disappeared into the background of whirring white noise and concentration that now-or-never thinking commands: "Be courageous, Luke. She waits for you. Be daring."

I inhaled several times to oxygenate my blood and become activated for this plunge at sixty-three miles an hour, pulling my arms behind me as if an artistic high diver...and then *leapt* as the eighteen-wheeler thundered by the jump spot, shattering the speed limit. Draft off the truck flung rocks, and a microburst slammed my back as I achieved apogee, pushing me into an awkward freefall, legs and arms flailing to restore vertical posture. I had learned much about the human body suspended in three-dimensions, but I was teetering too far forward with seconds to correct my posture.

My mistress waited, waters parting, ninety-one feet below.

WARRIOR

May 2010, a hospice in Denver, Colorado

Enumerable tumors. Not a few. Not negligible. Enumerable.

That's what Dr. Sen told me, and even with months to comprehend grave CT scans of a damaged and deteriorating liver, I still cannot fully grasp two fatal words: enumerable tumors.

I have spent fifty-seven years running from enumerable tumors—or from even a single tumor—metaphorically and literally. I have run thousands of miles: through parks and forests, along sidewalks and city streets. I have run, and for most of my life I have run triumphant, ripped and resolute. I have run since hearing the words "neurogenic sarcoma" uttered from my mother's lips—strange words I could not repeat or understand but words adding meaning to the lump on my neck that had grown golf-ball size in months. Some would call this a defining moment. You're eight, you're in military school—a brutal context where suffering can be snuffed out by adolescent bravado and disdain for differences—and lumps are ignored until golf-ball size.

I have run from heart disease and obesity and weakness. I have run from corporate orthodoxy and bad men hiding behind great power. I have run from more than a few lovers and momentary glimmers of not running fast enough: fears of failure, resignation, or banality. I have run from an eight-year-old surrendering to monumental pain and the indignities of not measuring up, and most assuredly, I have run from boredom, and in running from all this, I have run to wellness and a deeper sense of control over destiny.

I am in a peaceful yet final place now, a hospice in southeast Denver. I am resting on my deathbed as I jot down these thoughts. Deathbed. An idea anathema to the stories and adventures behind me. It's a comfortable bed: not hospital-like but homelike, a bed you might sleep in at a fine bed & breakfast, yet a bed hiding adjustment functionalities, so nurses and attendants can change mattress height and angle as my dependencies and care needs wax and wane.

A hospice might make you think of mushy vegetables, lime Jell-O, and catheters. Although my several hospital visits during the last few months have included those gustatory and penile humiliations, there is none of that here. I even ate a small salad two days ago, a garden on a plate filled with freshly picked vegetables and roasted nuts and feta cheese. They advised me to stay away from roughage with a deteriorating digestive system, but how else am I supposed to take a decent shit after ingesting so many opioids? To their credit, they'll fulfill almost any request here, and they refuse to remind me of my impending death with unnecessary machines, antiseptic odors, or mundane food, carelessly processed, microwaved, and rendered tasteless. They know me well enough to understand how important healthy food has been to me.

My caveman's diet—way ahead of its time in the modern era—plus thousands of miles of jogging paths have spared me from enumerable tumors, although those tissue demons have quietly haunted me for all these last fifty-seven years. I'm sixty-five now, so that's how long I've been pushing back, willing myself to overcome any obstacle, determined to live on my terms and not with the threat of some goddamn disease that scared the crap out of a small boy trying to survive military school in a brutal time, sometimes ignored by his Las Vegas entertaining mother but loving and idolizing that beautiful woman.

I'll try to keep anger out of this as much as possible but know that anger has been my friend and ally. You must be mad at cancer to survive fifty-seven years, but you cannot become obsessed by enumerable tumors. You must be angry at the forces that suppress and molest human beings, primarily the seven deadly sins: wrath, greed, sloth, pride, lust, envy, and gluttony.

But I'm getting ahead of myself, which is easy to do when you become clear that this could be your last month, week, or day. As you get to know me, you'll come to understand that I've been very good at slaying greed, sloth, envy, and gluttony. But wrath, pride, and lust have been more of a challenge. So, who's perfect? All I have ever asked is to be better today than I was a year ago: *progress not perfection*, as recovering substance abusers intone.

Other rooms have been filled with frail people breathing their final breaths like me. It's difficult for me to walk down the halls and pass these rooms, but at least these fading patients are not alone. These degenerating human bodies are usually surrounded by guests, family members, and benevolent volunteers. This is a hospice brimming with sunlight and optimism, fulfilling days against all odds, and overflowing with flowers and cheerful visitors and promises kept and unconditional positive regard and dignity.

It is a good place to die even if it is never a good day to die.

Pushing my intravenous apparatus ahead, I walk the halls daily, sometimes for more than merely minutes when I can stand the pain in my abdomen and joints. I am so weakened now that running is completely out of the question.

How does a concert pianist adapt to hands terrorized by arthritis? How does a pilot accept being grounded because he can no longer clearly see cockpit instruments in front of him? How does a towering man once the epitome of fitness—11 percent body fat and a body builder's physique—accept sarcopenia before his time? How does he accept muscle wasting due not to aging but to the ravages of enumerable tumors—hundreds of foreign bodies replacing healthy tissue with mutations of DNA, metastases mobilized beyond human control?

I won't apologize for these digressions. I hope you'll allow me that and not submit to a temptation to think of me as merely narcissistic. I've had to devote a lot of energy to fighting my shape-shifting nemesis, but I have loved and been loved, and this journey of mine is about much more than me. I hope you'll discover that my story is about your future choices.

I have tried my best to change the world, so to understand me is to understand ironic contrasts. I was a sickly, weak boy out of place in a military school in 1953. I was a football and track star in high school, lettering in both sports. I was a cancer survivor before puberty and then a Marine who trained on Parris Island for Vietnam. I was a misfit who found fitness. And a man who distrusted most men but loved some women beyond words sufficient to describe such devotions. I was a Doctor of Philosophy, twice, with double degrees in sports psychology and exercise physiology. I was a student of the mind with a mentally ill sister. I was a son without a father but restored by a grandmother who filled me with determination and health food sufficient to survive a difficult childhood. I was a lover with no commitment to any one woman and then a father of two beautiful young ladies from different mothers, offspring whom I love today as much as anyone or anything. I was a loner who found a soul mate, a fitness pioneer confronting a McDonald's Big Mac mentality at the apex of the Golden Arches power surge. I was a nonsmoker overcome with lung cancer. A Lothario diminished by prostate cancer. A passionate health and fitness public speaker whose voice was almost silenced by thyroid cancer.

I have faced death thirty-eight times throughout my life and survived, and now Thanatos will finally win—in weeks, days, or hours. During reflective moments that occupy my days here at Denver Hospice, I write this testimony and, in its telling, perhaps you will learn some lessons that I've discovered about living more fully. No time remains for secrets; what I must share about survival is yours. Use it or lose it.

I've beaten disease, depression, disinterest, and monotony. I've found the full expression of me through my running shoes and countless T-shirts drenched with sweat. I've defied aging, not to deny the inevitable but to thwart its pace, to beat it to the finish line. I have won countless confrontations with myself and maybe this knowledge will give you more time to be productive or diminish the losses that will inevitably send you to a hospital or hospice. That's really what I've accomplished: life on my terms.

I have been sitting on the edge of my bed, willing myself to stand and push the IV so that I can walk the halls. With so much swelling in my legs, I look out of balance, my once-upon-a-time ripped arms now frail, flaccid, and massless. I push into the bathroom to relieve myself, watching a stream that looks like Coca-Cola, a reminder that bilirubin is not breaking down in a liver confounded by enumerable tumors, also contributing to my jaundiced skin color. In the mirror, I look ten years older than my real age after a lifetime of always appearing ten years younger.

My feet want to drag, but I compel them to lift me into the hallway as if I'm marching to a classic rock band hidden in an orchestra pit below. I'm in the spotlight where I belong—strong and agile, a threatening persona to some, an alluring attraction to others—the way it always has been. I nod and smile at several young ladies who populate this place, recalling second looks that once frequently came my way. I think of myself as brown not yellow-orange; the women once saw me as a fitness devotee, more robust than other men. I'm a bit unusual here since most of the patients are chronologically ten-to-thirty years older.

"You look ... good today, Dr. Luke," assures nubile Heidi. She gives me a sincere smile and a nod of empathy and rushes down the hallway toward some unknown emergency. I wonder if it's another denizen dying but will not follow to investigate. I don't need that intense reminder of my own destiny, not now in the middle of a sunny May afternoon. It's not a good day to die.

Heidi and others call me Dr. Luke in honor of my academic achievements, but they never refer to me by my surname. Maybe that would be too formal in a place of dying where they work so hard to keep the atmosphere casual.

"Having lunch in our dining room?" asks Helen Jones, the nurses' supervisor.

"What's cooking?"

She glances at a nearby menu. "Baked white fish or pasta marinara."

"I'm not doing great with protein."

"Whatever sounds good...let us know."

"Maybe a smoothie for carbs and antioxidants." Okay...it's ridiculous to be thinking about anticancer foods when my body is ravaged with cancers. Old habits die hard, as do I.

Helen adds, "That might be better than solid food."

"You're right: It's a bit tough for me today."

She looks at me with kindness, perhaps some concern. "Pain is not allowed here. You tell us if your abdominal cramps become unbearable again."

"Okay. I'm going out now."

"You go, Dr Luke!" she declares with a fist pump. And she means it. She's a fitness buff herself with a lithe middle-aged body, the kind of physique you might encounter in someone who plays tennis a lot.

Pushing through pain and stiffness that is my new normal, I head outside to rest in the beautiful garden that they keep blooming April through October. Others who are ambulatory will take it easy in the garden also. It's hot outside, now more so with global warning sapping the planet's health, but frail bodies with poor circulation often appreciate added warmth. I hope for more than warmth; I want to sweat bullets because it's the one natural way I can help rid my body of surplus bilirubin.

It takes me seventeen more seconds to reach their garden than it did yesterday, but I finally push my way into the garden, IV in tow, notebook in my free hand. Nobody else is here given that it's early afternoon and the May sun is intense. Pink, red, and orange roses add flourish and fragrance to a restful spot. A redbud tree adds shade, as if a giant green umbrella blocking an intense blast of sunlight. But I choose a cement bench still in sunshine; I relish the warmth and have never worried about skin cancer of all the possible recurring threats of metastases that have hung over me through life as swords of Damocles. I have naturally brown skin and have soaked up more than my share of rays, from regular daytime runs through Washington Park to building redwood decks on the side. I love sunbeams. Let the sunshine in.

Noonday light also brings radiance to my orange-yellow skin, now almost golden as if a Titan, yet I am haunted by some cold ghosts of my past with which I will reconcile. Some poor choices and most of all, wrath. The puppies never stop screaming in my worst memories. So, I've been an angry man, and it's time to own the truth and accept who I have been.

Even with my foibles—and what mortal lacks them? —I am prepared to tell you that I have risked often. I have faith that I did fulfill my purpose for being here, and that I am finishing as a champion in the game of life. I hope you'll agree.

Chapter 2

NEMESIS

November 1952, Kansas City, Missouri

I hate Luke, every fiber of his being. I hate every bone, blood vessel, organ, and muscle. I hate what he thinks and how he feels, and it's my sublime pleasure when I can take over his consciousness and become the only thing that occupies his thoughts and feelings.

I hate his exuberance, playfulness, and the fact that he loves professional sports—even dreams of becoming a quarterback for a major football team or a track-running sensation. I loathe the life force bubbling through his arteries and veins and the meticulously complicated wiring of his muscles with nerves.

I like him when he's asleep and it's easier for me to get my job done, but I detest him during waking hours when he's busy being all boy: running around and being competitive with other growing boys like him.

Outsiders see a whole human being full of shouts and laughter and heartbeats and activities and curiosity and thoughtfulness and a touch of compassion. I see him as a piece of meat upon which I may dine and grow, commandeering his blood supply, gorging on glucose products from his digestive system, spreading myself like a web through connective tissues, muscle fibers, and nerves. Thousands of his tiny capillaries follow my commands and become my feeding tubes, allowing me to grow far more successfully than a growing boy. While his growth is symmetrical and intentional, known to follow predictable patterns and hallmarks, my enlargement is asymmetrical and unexpected, a deal breaker. I like it that way, the iconoclast of biological imperatives, the rambling rebel with a cause.

When you hate something or someone as much as I hate Luke, you plot, plan, and get even. And that is my singular focus and job. I'm very good at it.

Oncologists used to call me *neurogenic sarcoma*, which is a clinical name robbing me of dignity as a true and fearsome enemy of human longevity, a given name that's a futile attempt to objectify me and render my destructive ways more emotionally manageable and technically accessible. Or so they think.

More "modern" oncologists call me a *malignant peripheral nerve sheath tumor*, which demands an acronym here: MPNST. Simply stated, I begin in mutated cells located in a nerve, and the nerve I've picked is in Luke's neck. From there I grow, expand, and dominate.

Why, you wonder, did I choose Luke, an eight-year-old boy who hasn't hurt anyone or anything, a sensitive, intense child? That's an origin story worth retelling.

How I began my journey of domination over this boy remains a great mystery, but some hypothesize that my beginning can be related to overexposure to radiation. Maybe this boy breathed in too many of the winds rushing through the great plains from nuclear weapon test sites in Nevada and New Mexico when fallout floated across midwestern states, silently poisoning the air in a way not perceptible to human sensory organs. Their technologies measured troublesome levels of radiation and then dismissed the threat in a great cover-up, which is typical of a deceitful species. Those in power seldom reveal their full arsenal and neither do I.

A boy who loves to run and scramble and play outdoors could have inhaled more than his share of radioactive breezes, setting off a small detonation of growth known now as me, MPNST. That possibility aside, and given the rarity of a specimen like me, another alternative is more probable.

You see, when Luke was an infant, mostly wailing lungs demanding a bottle, a bacterial infection invaded his nasal sinuses. After many unsuccessful attempts to rid the child of those attacking pathogens, his attending physicians (my progenitors) landed upon a brilliant but untested strategy. They decided to deliver an unfiltered dose of X-ray radiation, aiming the poisonous rays at his neck and head. This indeed got the job done, so they thought. The unfortunate bacteria didn't have a chance, and the critters succumbed to a quick death from those invisible rays. You could think of what happened to Luke's sinuses as an analog for a 1950s-science fiction movie: extraterrestrial aliens with forbidding ray guns invade the planet and wipe out all who dare confront them, dominating the technologically deficient species they have chosen to colonize.

It took a few years for me to arise from the potentiality of Luke's damaged cellular DNA, but arise I did—at first slowly, imperceptibly, just a tiny mass of tissue below the skin of his neck, about halfway between his ear lobe and shoulder. A busy boy and those charged with his care wouldn't think of me as an enemy gaining a foothold if they could have discovered me through a more critical examination. His mom was too busy; his dad was nowhere to be found.

Luke was a peripatetic boy struggling to survive a difficult childhood in a military school run more like a World War II boot camp, and not only was he too distracted to notice me at first, so was the ignoramus school doctor who had given him a cursory physical examination.

I was much too small to be alarming to an overworked general practitioner with dozens of boys to examine and approve or disapprove for admittance. Maybe the harried doctor noticed me in my infancy, a tiny, nondescript bump, but thankfully he dismissed me as an irrelevant cyst or other benign abnormality. Let's also face facts: tumors of my stature capable of consuming a child are extraordinary indeed, and most doctors back then were unacquainted with my breed. Ignorance and carelessness are friends of an invading army.

I found my home in Luke's brachial plexus, a network of nerve fibers running from his spine through his neck and armpits and into his arms. My chosen command post had a very valuable role in the life of this boy since that nerve complex is responsible for skin and muscular innervations of the upper limbs.

But my clandestine assaults could not persist forever, though I relished my status as a guerilla attacker, dark and hidden from my enemy, exacting a toll before the enemy even understood the havoc that I brought. But lesions like me can lead to functional impairments, and eventually I made myself known to my young host through aching pain in his neck and jaw and then some gradual limitations of arm movement.

Since Luke is right-handed with much promise for athletic accomplishments after maturity, my right-side invasion made more sense to me: hit him where you can hurt him the most, my motto.

Timid and reticent about authority, unwilling to complain, fearing the consequences, Luke endured my growing dimensions and interference with his comfort and activities. Even as I grew from button size to nearly golf-ball size, he didn't complain, not to his mother who was then far away and busy as an entertainer in Las Vegas, and certainly not to that inept doctor.

My goal was to make myself known only when I had successfully dug my tendrils into all the tissues possible: nerve networks, muscles, connective tissues, fat deposits, and blood vessels, ideally the large vessels that supplied blood to his brain so that to excise me would probably end his life pronto. We're all going to die, but I like to choose my time and place. I like to be the last aggressor standing on the battlefield, triumphant, before my time to decay arrives.

So here I am, young fellow, golf-ball size and messy, with my duplicating tendrils spreading through your tissues as tunnels in an anthill. My hatred for you is pure and simple: to grow, to dominate, and to kill my host, the final demonstration of DNA gone haywire. My birth, growth, and blossoming are defiance personified for an arrogant species convinced that its technologies can grant eighty or ninety years of robust living. I am the ultimate foil against those miraculous human inventions like X-ray radiation that promise earlier diagnosis and longer lives.

Luke, my boy, your only hope for survival is complete surgical excision of all that is me, with very wide margins around me into healthy surrounding tissues, and I've truly made a mess of things. This means at the very least that you'll lose critical parts of you needed to function like a normal boy. If your surgeons miss any of me, even the most negligible microscopic essences,

I'll eventually recur where I started, or you can count on far-flung metastases—my distant cousins—in other hidden places where you least expect them.

Welcome to either your demise soon enough or a future dominated by waiting for me to poke up my ugly, beautiful head once again. Go to sleep, Lukey boy.

Go to sleep, useless child.

October 1953, University of Kansas Medical Center, Kansas City, Kansas

Note to reader: I vividly recall what it was like to be a child waking up from anesthesia to a damaged and surgically repaired body, becoming conscious of physical disabilities. So, I reconstruct that horrifying time from a boy's point-of-view, like this:

When I woke up I was dizzy, like riding on the Whirligig real fast. I didn't even know where I was. They told me I was okay and then I threw up in a pan. Everything looked white. Then I remembered myself and found my mind. It was kind of weird not to know who you are.

I knew I was eight. Eight years and seven months. Close enough to be nine. Bruce had turned ten one month before me, but I was almost as tall as him.

I had tried to be big and not let them see me cry. My head hurt really bad. So did my neck and arm. My neck hurt most. They told me it wouldn't hurt for long.

I couldn't move my arm or turn my head to look at a kid in the bed next to me. He didn't say much anyway. He slept all the time. They had wrapped me up in gauze like the mummy. The nurse showed me in a mirror because my mom had left on an airplane the night before, or she would have showed me.

All I could see was my eyes, nose, and mouth. Gauze was wrapped around my head and neck and chest and arm. I looked like a mummy in that movie with Boris Karloff. He was the scariest monster I ever saw. I didn't close my eyes even once when some of us guys went to the movies to see the *Creature from the Black Lagoon*. Who can fear a fishy man? We thought he was funny.

The Mummy was my favorite horror movie. I watched it on TV with Bruce. He was my best friend. He made french fries from real potatoes right in his kitchen, so we could eat them with ketchup when we watched the movie. His mom went to bed, so we watched it all alone with the lights off. We'd stayed up later than midnight!

We talked about staying up all night, but Bruce fell asleep in the TV room after that weird pattern came on the TV set and you couldn't watch anything else. I had to wake him up and push him to his room. I looked under the bunk bed twice to be sure the mummy wasn't under there. He teased me for being a scaredy cat. I liked Frankenstein better after that. Boris Karloff was that monster too. So, it was just the same.

They told me I had to look like a mummy for a long time. I couldn't move my arm or turn my head because the gauze they had wrapped me in was stiff. The nurse helped me eat dinner even though I could move my other arm and hand, but I wasn't very good at it. She promised it would get easier with practice. I wasn't hungry much anyway.

They told me the lump was gone forever, but they took out some muscles from my neck. I asked to see my lump, but they threw it away. I didn't believe them. Dr. Sawyer said I must practice but I could be almost like I was before he took out the lump. I had to go to special classes to help me get stronger.

I was getting strong before the operation. I could run faster than Bruce. One day I did ten whole pushups. He could only push up two times.

I felt tired and not very strong after the operation. I worried that kids at school would tease me for being a Caspar Milquetoast. Some of them didn't like me much because I didn't hang around with them. They weren't nice to me like Bruce.

Sarge Deville had tried to beat me up in the quad. He was a mean kid. After he pushed me down, I got up and hit him in the ear with my fist and he got bloody. I wasn't going to give up no matter what he did. Mr. Anderson stopped the fight and sent us both to detention. *But I didn't start it!* Sarge told me he was going to get even with me someday.

Nobody was going to beat me up when I got out of there. Bruce's dad had a York barbell set in their basement. That was the best barbell they made. When Bruce saw me at the hospital, he told me we could use it together. He promised and crossed his heart and hoped to die. He said we could eat lots of peanut butter. That's supposed to make you much stronger. I always liked peanut butter and grape jelly on toast. Bruce said Charles Atlas ate lots of peanut butter. I was not going to grow up and be a ninety-seven-pound weakling like the comic book ad said even though I was about ninety-five pounds right after the operation. Maybe I was less because they cut out the lump and other stuff. I didn't know for sure if that stuff weighs much. The nurse brought me a peanut butter sandwich for lunch one day like she promised.

There was a tube coming from under my arm. Yellow-reddish gunk came out all the time. The nurse changed the bag thing and left the tube stuck in me. There was another tube stuck in me, and it kind of hurt but not as much as my neck. Bruce peeked under the sheets. He teased me that it was stuck up my weewee. I got mad at him for looking at my private parts. They said they would take it out when I could get out of bed and go to the bathroom all by myself. I didn't go number two for days. They called it a new word—constipation. I worried about what they would do when I had to go number two and was stuck in a bed. The guy nurse told me to let them know when I had to go number two. I held it in as long as I could.

I knew right then that I would never let Sarge Deville beat me up. That was for sure. I was not going to let any kid beat me up ever again. I'm a fighter when someone pushes me around. My big sister was too nutso to stick up for me. She either laughed so much she couldn't stop or yelled bad things at people. I didn't like to be around Joanne. I learned I had to take care of myself as soon as the doctor let me. So, when I got out of that horrible hospital I lifted York barbells almost every day and ate lots of peanut butter with Bruce.

Chapter 3

LOVER

November 1986, a hotel swimming pool in Denver, Colorado

She wrapped me in her embrace, sensuous, dreamy, reassuring. She had become my truest friend at that moment, the one who nurtured me and helped keep my anxieties under control. I had grown accustomed to her soft predictability. While remaining mysterious and alluring, she had become so familiar after nearly two days of constant immersion in her depths. She was wet, warm, constant, ever-present—my whole world.

To those standing on her edges and looking down at us, she was nothing more than a swimming pool in a hotel on Colorado Blvd. But to me she was everything that mattered in my compressed life. She surrounded me and dominated everything I saw and felt. I embraced her with all my being because for two days our relationship followed the trajectory of a love affair: exuberant at first, full of mystery and enchantment. Then doubts and disillusionment in the darkest hours of night. And then full of hope again as morning sunlight beamed from skylights above to cause her to shimmer and glimmer, reminding me of the ephemeral, the transitory nature of our relationship and the possibilities for a mature mutual understanding as time passed. She could lull me into peaceful bliss as if I were in amniotic fluid where the problems of life float away. She could also be a vixen, threatening and controlling, reminding me that with one wrong move I risked death through suffocation.

It was late in my second day fully submerged in a hotel pool without a break or interruptions. Media interest in my budding celebrity as a daredevil had nearly reached a crescendo, so the hotel owners had allowed my crew and me to take over the pool for as many days as I could stand being continuously submerged without leaving her underwater lair. I was vaguely committed to beating a world record if possible, but that could not be my singular motivation. The record was far off into the distant future, back then owned by an underwater diving expert. I was but a novice, having just passed my scuba diving certification less than a month earlier. Life under water for me was an alien experience. I'm ambitious, of course, but I was also realistic about my chances.

I had exceeded the owners' expectations, and I doubt that they regretted their decision to accommodate my experiment. Reporters came and went. Photos had been taken—a few underwater. The previous day's photo of me toasting the camera with a champagne glass from the depths of the pool, outfitted in my scuba equipment, had landed in the newspaper on the front page. Whoopee! I was suddenly a Rocky Mountain celebrity. Television crews covered my feat for an evening news report, capturing interest from the public, and then a gaggle of curious onlookers hung around the pool observing my silent underwater vigil while speculating on how and when I'd quit. Bets were being taken.

My feet screamed with pain, the cumulative effects of chlorine slowly digesting me as if a diluted acid. That had been my biggest mistake thus far. Every time I did one of these feats I treated it as a complex problem to be solved. I considered every variable, and then I often sought advice from notable experts to guide further planning and preparations. I should have insisted that the hotel drain the pool and refill it with fresh water. But we would have been pushing our luck to get exclusive access to the pool for an unspecified number of days without incurring refilling costs. Okay, we had not anticipated how chlorine reacts to skin after many hours of submersion. You may recall how chlorine and water eventually wrinkled your skin when you swam for hours as a child, but those wrinkles turn into burning chasms of unbelievable pain when you remain in pool water long enough. The sunburn-like pain, which I soon learned to manage through meditation, was a minimal distraction compared to other challenges. Nevertheless, I should have consulted with someone knowledgeable about the long-term effects of chlorinated pool water on human skin. I wrote a mental note to myself: *be vigilant about chemical and environmental interactions in the future.*

Keeping a mouthpiece firmly between my lips, especially when I swapped consciousness for brief moments of slumber, was something for which I could not have prepared ahead, though preparation was my middle name. I knew I would feel fatigue with accumulation of sleeplessness and the physical exertion required to remain submerged with my liquid lover. But soon I felt wasted, as if just finishing a multiday sexual marathon, all intensity and zeal spent through the climax. I wanted just to fall asleep for many days, if possible. But she was surrounding me, and she would not allow slumber except for brief moments of a waking, dreamlike state, and then my well-being was at risk again.

Psychological perils preoccupied me the most. During nearly forty-eight hours, I had at times been irritable, depressed, elated, joyous, and anxious. I had felt grave distrust of my crew, questioning their motives, doubting that they were facilitating my success. Superficiality and pretense cannot survive underwater if I did.

Peaceful classic rock music filled the underwater depths with reassurances. Embedded in the music, below the level of conscious awareness, affirming statements had been recorded. We called it subliminal communication, and clinical research had recently demonstrated that these subconscious statements could elevate confidence and tolerance of enormous frustration. Staying underwater in a confining swimming pool became the epitome of frustration.

I am whole and healthy.
I am in control of every moment.
The embracing water loves me.

These affirming statements hid below the threshold of perception in nostalgic songs from The Eagles, James Taylor, Carole King, and Fleetwood Mac. Hit songs from my college days had kept me attached to reality so my world did not become too dreamlike or bizarre. Embedded affirmations overwhelmed my tendencies to feel isolation and the sense of being caged as a wild animal. But my battles to tolerate the void of a never-ending submersion persisted, no matter our elaborate preparations—my extreme fitness or all the psych training I had accomplished.

More than anything else I hate boredom. That is why I'm unwilling to embrace a predictable, corporate lifestyle, where every day is much like the day before. Being contained in a twenty foot by fifty-foot pool became cage-like, or perhaps better said, fishbowl-like. Within a few hours of submersion, I encountered the *fishbowl effect*: the moments of perceived redundancy when I had already studied every corner and crack, every painted number or line. I had circled the pool more times than I could recall, soon knowing what to expect with every breaststroke or paddle. I had learned the cracks and crevices, the flaws and oversights of the pool constructors. I had tried somersaults and games with a rubber ball to distract me from the monotony of the same confining, repetitious space.

But boredom, my hated enemy, had caught up with me. And lurking behind boredom came resignation and regret. Then vulnerability. And paranoia.

I felt as if I was being watched by unknown eyes on the surface above. The watchers were my adversaries: they hoped I would fail and emerge from the depths before I had accomplished anything that mattered. Some of them expected that I'd drift into deep sleep, drop the mouthpiece, and inhale enough water to drown before my crew had time to rescue me. They secretly wished to witness a lifeless body being brought to the surface, confirming the validity of their miserable, over-eating, cigarette-smoking, television-addicted lifestyles.

Breaking news at ten!

My sensory-deprived state and my sense of vulnerability compelled me to retreat, quite thankfully, into a habitat that I had the foresight to include in this experiment. Constructed from four fiberglass panels, my habitat was about double the size of a typical coffin, an appropriate metaphor, I guess. It sat at the deepest end of the pool, farthest from the surface, about ten feet below. When I felt overwhelming vulnerability, I swam inside my underworld home and hid from invading eyes and flaw-seeking cameras. There my liquid lover and I could enrapture each other in fantasies of lust and love.

My watch announced 3:04 a.m. of the second night, approaching thirty-two hours underwater. And the habitat that hid me from insensitive gawkers above also amplified my profound sense of isolation from my fellow humans. I was ready to quit and signal the attending team psychologist that I wanted to end the experiment and surface, as we had agreed in advance. I could not endure another minute in that pool.

Rob did his job, for which I paid him a substantial consulting fee as a clinical psychologist with nationally renowned expertise in sensory deprivation. He signaled Jody, my flesh and blood love, my sweetheart. Through the dim light above I saw the shadowy outline of a lithe, athletic female body as my team outfitted her with a scuba tank and facemask. In moments, she slipped into the water and swam down to me where I waited just outside my habitat. When she reached me, she embraced me with her long arms and legs wrapped around me, as she had done so often during our sexual escapades. We could not kiss because of the awkward mouthpieces and goggles, but we embraced as if reliving the first moments of our blossoming love for each other. Her presence, so reassuring, lulled me into memories of sweet bygone moments. My liquid lover mattered no more, and I became transported away from monotony, vulnerability, and fear. I became transported.

Two years earlier, July 1984, Denver, Colorado

I was jogging along E. Seventh Avenue in Denver, a few blocks east of Colorado Blvd., following my normal route toward Quebec Street. The wide, tree-lined residential street, framed by stately minimansions, was verdant in mid-July and during that late evening, quite peaceful.

I appeared to be an unusual specimen in my bright red nylon jogging shorts, which nevertheless revealed the shape of my manhood—or so I had been told more than once. I was wearing those scant shorts with an old olive-green Marines T-shirt—one of my favorite mementos from my thirteen weeks of grueling training at the Parris Island Marine Corps Recruit Depot. That had been where I learned to love running so much because recruits are required to run everywhere, seemingly mandated to cover all 8,095 acres every never-ending week.

We ran from our sleeping quarters to the mess to the shooting range and then back again. We ran from the Iwo Jima Monument to the Molly Marine Monument and then to the Iron Mike Monument. We ran way too often around the perimeter of the Legends Golf Course, wary of incoming golf balls smacked carelessly—or not—by commanding officers. We even ran to the Brig 'n' Brew for the occasional but blessed sedation of a cold one.

From this hellhole of physical stress and mental intimidation, I had received in return that which I so deeply needed as a young man: extreme fitness and combat readiness. Little did they know—because they would have rejected me in a heartbeat—that I was a cancer survivor; thankfully they did not dig deep enough into my childhood health records. *Semper Fi*.

I was not wearing socks but merely sneakers from a new public company called Nike, named after the Greek goddess who personifies winning. I was not convinced that these new shoes were well designed for someone who ran at least thirty miles every week, as I did, but I loved the swoosh metaphor for strength, speed, and victory. Besides, they had mailed me a free trial pair after they read about my bridge jump. The marketing people had hoped I would add my name to a list of celebrity endorsers. *Who me? A celebrity?* That was going to take some time to believe.

In a moment of profound appreciation, I sensed the mystical beauty of this instant in time as I always did about three or four miles into my daily run. Birds were chirping. Kids were playing in a few front yards. The temperature had lowered from a high of ninety-five degrees to somewhere in the low eighties.

A young man, a teenager, was mowing a lawn in front of a house just a hundred yards ahead. He spotted me and stopped to ponder this anomaly. A man running? From what? I could see what was going on in his head. Joggers were so infrequent a spectacle that sometimes people stopped and wondered if they were nut cases or criminals fleeing the scene of a felony. Nevertheless, I smiled and waved at him as I passed his house. He responded with a weak wave, as if uncertain about whether he should acknowledge some weirdo in bright red nylon running shorts who towered over him by six or seven inches. Parris Island instilled in me both a love of running and a body that could easily belong—and don't think I'm being self-absorbed here—to another Greek god named Adonis. I looked attractive to women and intimidating to many men, but I was quite comfortable in my skin because I had worked so hard to hone my physique while strengthening my resolve never to be out of shape for the rest of my life.

I continued my easy stride across Quebec Street, barely pausing to negotiate the rush of traffic from both directions. Once on the other side of that busy intersection, I continued east on Seventh until I reached Roslyn Street, where I took a left, aiming toward E. Eighth and eventually Crescent Park. I loved to include that small park in my daily runs, enjoying the evening interplay between lovers strolling, dogs chasing Frisbees, and children running around like little monkeys, liberated and spirited.

The sun had almost set with dusk beginning to settle over Denver, the crimson light adding a sense of drama and mystery. How glorious and inexplicable our lives are, we mere mortals, capable of god-like deeds but imprisoned in temporality. On the walls of a stately brownstone ahead I saw what appeared to be flashing lights. This startled me because it was so unexpected to see red-and-blue lights pulsating off the walls of a residential home. I glanced over my shoulder to see a police car with his strobe lights assaulting the peaceful bliss that I had been experiencing. I continued running north and his car crawled behind me. I sped up into more of a lope, and he accelerated the cruiser to keep pace with me. Finally, he issued a blast of the squad car siren, a squeal demanding that I must stop running and pull over.

A rotund, middle-aged man stepped out of the squad car and approached me, a disapproving glare. Thirty pounds' overweight with a potbelly hanging over his belt, he looked as if he hadn't worked out in years. He was anathema to every value I cherish.

"What are you doing?" he demanded.

"Jogging."

"What do you mean ... *jogging*?"

"I am an exercise physiologist and sports psychologist. I run to stay fit...and for fun."

He furrowed his eyebrows. "We received a call from a concerned citizen in this neighborhood. There have been robberies around here recently. She believes you could have committed a crime."

"As I've told you, officer, I am running for recreation and fitness. It's a hobby."

"Nobody runs for a hobby. That's ridiculous." The cop glowered. "What are you running *from*?"

Scanning his girth, I imagined the damage he had already done to his circulatory system. His coronary arteries could be packed with plaque. I had seen coronary angiographies of men similar in girth to this police officer. Out of shape men like him can be one more plate of Fettuccini Alfredo away from a massive myocardial infarction.

"I asked, what are you running *from*?"

I scanned his obese body, matching his repugnant expression and answered, "Heart disease!" He looked dumbfounded. "I am *running* from heart disease!"

"Don't you even think about being a smartass, or I'll take you to the station for questioning."

"You have no grounds to detain me, officer, because I'm a law-abiding citizen. I have never committed a crime. I'm enjoying one of our many freedoms as Americans: the privilege to run when I please in a city where I pay taxes."

"Show me your I.D."

"Where do you think I'd carry an I.D.? All I have is a house key."

"The law requires you to show identification if I suspect you've been involved in illegal activity."

Enough is enough. "Excuse me officer, are you detaining me or am I free to go?"

He looked around the area as if trying to discover evidence of a burglary or assault. But, of course, his ridiculous inquiry was unwarranted. "All right, I'll let you go. But you find some other neighborhood for your jogging from now on. A homeowner near here does not appreciate seeing you running half-naked through this area. I'm responding to a complaint."

"Residents will see more runners like me because jogging is catching on everywhere. It's becoming a huge fitness trend."

"Homeowners deserve privacy."

"Recreational running is a trend. It won't be so unusual to see many men and women running during the evenings or mornings. You should give it shot..."

"Just do as I order. I will detain you for further questioning if I receive another complaint. People around here are suspicious of strangers running through their neighborhood."

"Seriously, do I look like a threat to you?"

"You're barely dressed."

"It's summer and hot as hell!"

"What is that Marines shirt you're wearing?"

My well-developed pectoral muscles made the shirt look more forceful, so I paused to make a point before answering. "I was a Marine. Honorably discharged as a lance corporal after three years of service. A Vietnam veteran..."

"You dishonor the corps with those fag shorts."

37

"Who are you to judge what I wear or my service? If you're not going to detain me, then this conversation is over."

I began stepping backward, still facing the officer, staring with stern authority at the cop, a military bearing I had learned on the battlefield, confident that my innate capacity to intimidate had been successful. "And you should be jogging to prevent the heart attack that's coming your way if you don't take better care of yourself."

The cop grumbled something unintelligible and waved me off as if an irritating peon. I turned again and just as a healthy animal I ran purposefully, more certain of my path than ever.

One life, one body, one chance to get it right. Now or never.

Crescent Park beckoned me as I approached, and there I stopped for a moment to catch my breath and reflect upon the silliness of my confrontation with the policeman. I was not very winded but with miles behind me I was aware that even Luke must rest to recharge for the run home. I fully intended to run through the same neighborhoods that inspired my unsavory encounter with Mr. Fat Cop.

Just a few yards ahead of me, I was struck by the visage of a young woman, also in a jogging-style outfit, sexy and clingy. She was touching her toes as if stretching out for a run. I ambled over, mindful that I must appear loose and easygoing because my size and chiseled features could threaten those who didn't know me.

"You look like you might be a runner," I offered in a soft voice with a reassuring smile.

She looked up, maybe a bit startled, and smiled back. "Yes. I started running about two months ago, at the start of summer. Nothing else makes me feel as energized."

"It's the endorphins."

"The what?"

"Endorphins. Opioid peptides that function as neurotransmitters. The pituitary gland and hypothalamus produce them during exercise. We also manufacture them when we feel excitement or pain, eat spicy food, and...during lovemaking. Endorphins resemble opiates because they can reduce pain and create a feeling of well-being."

Any initial disinterest in her demeanor melted away; her eye contact became more engaging. So, I continued, "That's what you feel during and after a good run: perhaps a deeper sense of peace."

"You know your stuff," she said. "Are you a jock?"

Without appearing to be an obvious lecher, I took in her tall physique, which was as lean as an athlete's. She must have been nearly six feet tall. Her proportions were perfect: breasts neither too big nor too small. Her tanned legs were sinewy and strong, with prominent calf muscles. She couldn't be more that 20 percent body fat.

"My name is Luke." I reached out my hand and she took it, shaking firmly as if at a business meeting.

"I'm Jody."

"Wow, strong handshake."

"Are you an athlete?" she pressed.

"I'm an exercise physiologist and sports psychologist."

"What do you do?"

"Well, I started Denver's first heart-monitored cardiac rehabilitation center. We help heart attack victims recover from surgery, so they can hopefully resume the lives they had before being stricken. How about you?"

"I'm an intensive care nurse at University Hospital. It looks as if we have both chosen medical fields. And here we are today, staying fit."

Her eyes were wide and blue, the kind of ice-blue that's almost mesmerizing, especially because her eyes were framed by long black eyelashes. Her hair was brownish-blonde, natural in color and tied in a ponytail. Her running outfit was pure white with a few pink accents. "I just had an encounter with a very obese cop who thought I might be committing a crime because I was running."

"Was that you? I saw the flashing lights from his car but chose to ignore the distraction while I was running around the park. I get into a very Zen place when I run. Did he give you a ticket?"

I laughed so heartily I almost surprised myself, not being a frequent laugher. "That would be a first: getting a traffic ticket for exceeding the speed limit of five miles an hour."

She giggled also, showing beautiful teeth, white and straight. "How ridiculous! It sounds like you met the Texas sheriff from *Smokey and the Bandit*. You know…the character played by Jackie Gleason."

"You're right! Buford T. Justice! He fit the character to a tee."

She looked at me as if seeing me, taking in my broad shoulders and strong physique. Her eyes hesitated on the right side of my neck where surgeons had removed muscle, lymph glands, and nerve tissue, including my sternocleidomastoid muscle, which is responsible for assisting with head and neck rotation. Because of my extensive weight-training regimen to rebalance my physique, most people do not notice an absence of muscle mass and the slight tilt of my head, but Jody is a nurse and clearly knows her anatomy. The short lapse in our conversation caused an awkward moment.

She said, "Well, I should keep running before I cool down too much. I was just stretching out when you walked over."

"Which way are you running?"

"I'm heading back to my apartment near the hospital."

"That's close to my home next to City Park. How about running together?"

She hesitated a moment as if considering the risks and benefits. "Well, all right, Luke, but I need to split off from you before I reach home. We don't know each other and…"

"I understand perfectly, Jody. This is a chance encounter for both of us, but we have much in common. I'd love to learn more about your work in intensive care. That's a noble calling."

"I'm also interested in cardiac rehabilitation."

"Okay, it's a deal. Let's run and when we get close to your neighborhood you let me know, and I'll trot off another direction."

"Deal. You lead off. It looks as if you can set a challenging pace, and that's the way I like it."

"I'll keep it challenging but not to the point of breathlessness. I have questions for you." Trying not to be obvious, I again appreciated this incredible female form before me, her self-confidence and athleticism, an aura surrounding her. This was the woman of my dreams: sensuous, soft, and in shape.

Chapter 4

CRASH

June 2010, a hospice in Denver, Colorado

The days have stretched out as I hoped they would. Maybe that's the final gift of my life, a precious concluding chance for perspective and retrospective. That's what hospice means to me now...an almost painless chance to sum it all up, say the good-byes I need to say, and sail into the sunset knowing Life is over for me with nothing left to finish.

As I aged toward my current sixty-fifth year, it seemed that days, weeks, months, and years started to zip by faster with each new season. When I looked in the mirror, expecting to see the robust young man who jumped from the Paseo Bridge, I saw someone middle-aged, more haggard, but fit, as I promised myself decades ago. Looking again I saw a man whose curly mane of black hair was showing generous splashes of gray. Once when running toward the wide, tinted glass doors of an office building, suddenly in a reflection I saw a man who could be a grandfather. My only consolation then was also seeing the legs of a man with ripped quads, indistinguishable from a fit professional bicyclist. Time seems to force upon humans a cruel irony: the older we get, the faster it ticks away as the clock is winding down.

But now that I'm sixty-five and dying, the sun rises and sets in a week. A week has become a month. The flow of time in Denver Hospice is no longer clock-bound but circumscribed by thoughts and feelings and recollections and unrequited dreams. I am undistracted to travel the throughways and potholes of my mental life. I fill this time with these thoughts and stories.

I ate breakfast with Charlie today, just hours ago. Or rather, I should say, I ate, and he watched from his wheelchair. He is also here to die from a wretched malady called amyotrophic lateral sclerosis, or ALS, a disease of the nerve cells in the brain and spinal cord that control voluntary muscle movement. You probably have heard of it as Lou Gehrig's Disease for the legendary Yankee slugger and first baseman who was told in 1939 of his deteriorating destiny. He accepted the verdict with godly grace and died less than two years later; Lou was rounding the base to age thirty-eight. To me, it's Charlie's disease, a ghastly sentence to death that mollifies the few moments each day I allow for self-pity. Charlie's gift is a reminder that, while I'm living with a bum rap heading nowhere but an urn, I am blessed to be losing the battle with merely stage IV liver cancer.

Why am I so blessed? In ALS, nerve cells waste away or die and can no longer send messages to muscles. This eventually leads to muscle weakening, twitching, and an inability to move the arms, legs, and body. The condition gets worse with each week becoming more challenging.

Charlie came here before me, and he will probably survive me by weeks, maybe months. ALS is cruel in its lackadaisical pace, but in his situation the course of the disease seems to be aggressive. Charlie has an unusually fast-moving form, compressing a disease that can take years to kill into months. Maybe he's lucky or maybe not. I would ask Stephen Hawking, the eminent astrophysicist and author who lived with the disease for over fifty years, what he thinks—if he was accessible by spiritual e-mail.

Charlie's doctors give him less than six months, thus the right to receive support for palliative care paid for by Medicare and live out his final weeks or months in a hospice. But function by function, he is losing control of his body to eventually becoming a thinking brain connected to a pile of almost dead meat. He had no desire to stay at home and be a caregiving quandary for his wife and three adult children. That is one measure of a man's character: that he would choose to leave his home and live out his last days in unfamiliar surroundings, homelike though they may be. That's also why I'm not at my house now. Jody and my daughters do not need grisly memories of my deteriorating bodily functions and ebbing strength.

Charlie was also an athlete, though not with nearly as storied a career as the great homerun slugger Lou Gehrig, the namesake for his disease. Charlie played basketball for the University of Kansas and for his first season called Wilt "the Stilt" Chamberlain his teammate. He loved the game, performed brilliantly for KU, and might have made it onto the roster of a professional team but instead followed his father into the family law firm. He stayed involved in basketball through youth sports and became an accomplished coach.

Earlier this morning, Charlie displayed the ultimate measure of trust between two dying jocks. He spoke like his tongue was swollen to twice its normal size, yet he confided in me that he had considered suicide on several occasions, which I also have thought about quite a lot. It's most difficult to have lived in the body of someone so intimately acquainted with perfect health, raw physicality, and to then passively watch muscles wither, stamina disappear, and a lifetime of robust self-image crumble under the humiliating weight of one's own mortality, unambiguously on display by any mirror or a friend's shocked expression at the start of visitations. Charlie and I now know those demons too well.

That confession finished, Charlie then struggled to move a large spoon from an oatmeal bowl to his mouth, but he still insisted that nobody should help him even though he had already splattered his bib as if a food fight loser. I reached to help guide a spoon to his mouth and he threw it at me, though not with enough force to allow the spoon to travel the several feet between us. He knew that I understood his defiance and unwillingness to submit to any more assistance than absolutely required, and perhaps that ended the fight before it started. We're warriors in our own ways.

"How do you want it to end?" Charlie tongued as if a lisping, asthmatic drunk.

I thought for a moment, reviewing my large catalog of anatomical knowledge. "I guess that sometime in the night I just stop breathing and fly away forever."

"That will be how I die...stop breathing. Can't talk. Just take breath and stop. No re-suspiration-itation. Pneumonia probably."

"Same here. Perhaps we can coordinate the day and time?"

Charlie laughed at my ridiculous proposal and continued my thought. "Yes...generous. Call me on house phone...if your night to kick. I kick too."

We chuckled together with camaraderie that healthy people promised years of longevity can rarely understand. Death deserves only one response from lifelong fighters: irony and sarcasm. It's our human nature to laugh at what we cannot control—that which diminishes us from self-evolving, self-empowering beings, turning us into dust.

Dust in the Wind, as the rock supergroup Kansas intoned a generation ago. *All we are is dust in the wind.*

August 2001, a highway from Golden to Nederland, Colorado

At 5:30 a.m., I blasted from Boulder to Nederland on Highway 119 in mid-August, leaning into switchbacks, rounding curves. No helmet. Just blue jeans and a T-shirt and jacket. I wouldn't wear a helmet and biker leathers even though Jody refused to drop her nagging. She believes I've got a death wish, which is the opposite of the truth. I love life by seeking confrontations with myself when the sane choice is what everyone else thinks I should do and the crazy choice is tempting fate, which is what I always do.

Steep canyon walls echoed the throaty thunder of my Harley-Davidson Sportster with the 1200 cc V-Twin engine first introduced in 1988. This bike romps, filling the canyon with its signature calling card: *potato-potato-potato-potato-roar-potato-potato-roar*. Fuel injection nails down a sound that separates Harley from all foreign pretenders. The torque is tenacious as I glide through turn after turn with pure mechanical throb. I take pride in my ride's all-American heritage, a product born and bred on native soil, a brand that summarizes my freethinking proclivities punctuated by early morning rumble.

I was probably waking up some of the mountain denizens in far-flung cabins above 119, or Boulder Canyon Drive as the locals call it, but this was my primetime to ride. Sorry guys. Wind in my hair, chilly mountain air filling the canyons at dawn, a sense of connection to my ancestors who rode a similar bike back in the thirties, that's why I ride anytime I can: my time to sort it all out without needing to think about it too hard.

Flow time.

I pulled off the highway at Barker Reservoir. The small alpine lake reflected soft daybreak light. Two hundred paces from the turnoff I climbed a car-size boulder and sat above the silent waters, my senses alive with sharp odors of blue spruce and faint Canadian Geese honks from a migrating flock also waking with dawn. I had stopped there often to meditate and think about the future.

What am I trying to accomplish?

That's a reasonable question and one that Jody poses to me almost daily. Why am I taking risks with my life…to prove what? Good question, deserving better than the classic answer given by English mountain climber George Mallory when asked why he wanted to climb Mount Everest: "Because it's there."

I have chosen to undertake feats of endurance and physical challenge as experiments to test my theory that risk taking is one path to achieve optimum health and wellness. It may seem paradoxical at first thought: to assure a long, healthy life, humans need to take risks—physical challenges sufficiently demanding to push them out of habit, boredom, and comfort zones. My data supports significant baseline reductions of stress hormones such as adrenaline and cortisol, which, when chronically produced, have been associated with metabolic syndrome, heart disease, and impaired cognitive performance. Chronic stress shortens lives or makes them less productive; and modern, desk-bound workers steep their bodies in steady doses of cortisol because of deadlines, corporate politics, boot-licking, and unending demands to perform.

Another discovery has implications far into the future of sports medicine and wellness. Oxytocin is a neurotransmitter produced by our brains in reaction to the interpersonal bonding and trust that often happens as a byproduct of planning and undertaking feats. This molecule has the capacity to reduce stress—which is no minor matter when you consider the toll that stress takes on our bodies. Oxytocin reduces cortisol and lowers blood pressure. It can also improve digestion, which is often disturbed by high stress levels. It improves gut motility and decreases intestinal inflammation, meaning that we absorb nutrients better and become more efficient eating machines.

Although my experiments clearly increase cortisol and adrenaline production in reaction to short-term threats to my physical safety, my body also produces an abundance of endorphins and testosterone, which linger long after my experiments have been concluded. I've demonstrated that the relaxation response critical for a long and abundantly healthy life becomes optimally activated in those who have challenged themselves with risks, which I instruct must be managed with preparation, planning, and foresight.

It is quite a simple insight: take positive physical risks and live longer and healthier. Much more work needs to be undertaken so I can fully explain how chronic stress—the so-called *fight or flight response*—is destroying the health and viability of modern humans, even though the environment rarely calls upon us to fight or flee. This is just our body's physiological reaction to lives tied to computers and office cubicles with so much out of our control in a modern technological society. Our bodies respond as if we're being threatened by a wild animal or a neighboring tribal enemy, but we are only reacting to ambiguous expectations by supervisors, unrealistic needs from children, or time starvation due to so many overlapping deadlines. Our modern lives flood us with cortisol when we have no place to run and no individual to fight. We get angry and then we get depressed. Then we become couch potatoes and escape in front of a television, eating junk food and packing on too many pounds. Our phantom battles with modernity take a toll on health, and I have made it part of my life's mission to lure my friends and growing fan base from their sedentary, predictable, and unchallenging lifestyles.

I have also examined the concept of *flow*. Flow is unwavering immersion in activity—complete absorption—and the ultimate way to harness emotions in service of high-performance. My planned feats are always about flow. To achieve this state, I deconstruct each stunt into exquisite details, reassembling my problem as if a complex math equation until I reach a solution that guarantees survival. I map out each minuscule step to reach my objective. During the most dangerous moments of these experiments, my reward is the *flow experience*. My emotions become positive, energized, and aligned with my chosen risk. I command intense focus on nothing other than my chosen activity, freed from self-consciousness about my emotional musings in the moment—a loss of the reflective self-consciousness that inhibits most humans. Taoism has for millennia recognized this mindset as "action of inaction" or "doing without doing." I conquer self-doubts, depression, and anxiety as I achieve a transcendent state that some believe empowered Michelangelo as he painted the ceiling of the Vatican's Sistine Chapel. The pinnacle of the flow experience includes feelings of spontaneous joy, even rapture. Often achieved through calculated risk-taking, flow is a critical wellness strategy.

I don't undertake strenuous challenges, steeped with danger, because they are there. I push myself with the wisdom succinctly articulated by Friedrich Nietzsche, the nineteenth century existentialist and philosopher: "That which does not kill us makes us stronger." That which does not kill Luke makes me stronger, and I've been gaining strength with leaps and dives and dodges for most of my life.

While reflecting upon my evolving theories of wellness, the sun continued rising from behind mountains to my east, and pink alpenglow gradually filled the sky above me. I could see that the sun would soon peek around the mountains, and the pace of commuting traffic had picked up along Highway 119. I climbed down from my boulder perch and ambled back to my Harley. The motorcycle roared alive and rolled with confidence over the gravel turnout; goosing the accelerator sped me along the short remaining hop to Nederland.

The mountain town had been made famous by many recording artists from the 1960s and 1970s, especially one of my favorite troubadours, Dan Fogelberg, a multifaceted folk, rock, and pop artist who wrote and sang one of Jody's and my favorite love ballads, *Longer*: "Longer than there've been stars up in the heavens, I've been in love with you." His fourth album, released in 1977 when I finished my two doctoral degrees, is called *Nether Lands*, inspired by Nederland, where Fogelberg once lived and wrote some of his well-known songs, recording a few of them at nearby Caribou Ranch.

Still barely daybreak, with typical morning hubbub making the city streets seem busier, I rumbled into the city center, throttled down, traveled through shopping areas and around a roundabout, and turned on S. Bridge Street heading toward Rollinsville. That little dot on 119, about five miles from Nederland, is another small mountain town with a classic rock heritage. It's home to the Stage Stop Inn, a barbeque and bar that has hosted some famous rock 'n' roll luminaries, such as Joe Walsh of the Eagles and Stephen Stills of Crosby, Stills, and Nash. Rumors have lingered for decades that Stills got into a bar brawl there, and one drunken reprobate tossed him through a window. It was my ultimate destination for that morning ride, where, after a cup of java, I planned to detour on Highway 72 to return to the West Denver suburbs and then home, just as Jody would normally awaken to begin her day.

Once past First Street, I pushed the accelerator with confidence that the local constables were still in their beds. Jumping from 15 mpg to 45 mpg in a few seconds, ahead I saw a rickety black flatbed truck pulling out in front of me at S. Hendricks Street. The dude didn't even look; he just went for it. It was too late for me to stop before impact, and there was nowhere I could evasively turn to dodge the truck. I had no choice but to lay my Harley on the pavement with me partly beneath it, sliding under the truck. The Harley's rear wheel connected with the rear wheel of the truck, and the truck rolled over the rear Harley wheel, and both vehicles came to sudden stop. I felt extraordinary pain in my left rib cage as it connected with the right handlebar of the motorcycle, and my head snapped back to hit the pavement as morning light clicked off to midnight.

August 2001, Boulder County Hospital, Boulder, Colorado

"Luke. Luke, it's me."

I returned from a dark void with only a fuzzy sense of time and place. I almost instinctively knew I was in a hospital without seeing a lot of confirming details. Hospitals have been a continuing footnote in my life since early childhood. I can smell them with my eyes closed.

I forced my eyes open to a flood of artificial light and Jody's face near my own. I could see concern in her expression. Another person, perhaps a nurse, hovered nearby checking some equipment. "I'll inform his doctor," he said and left the area.

"Luke, you'll be okay. You've had an accident."

"Jesus. I remember. A damn trucker pulled out from a side street."

"That's right."

Suddenly I felt enormous pain in my left upper chest as if a knife was sticking from an area below my clavicle. My left leg hurt also. Raising my head, I could see right away that my lower leg had been encased in a white plaster cast. "How many bones?"

"Just your left fibula below the patella. You're lucky that way. A clean break. It should heal rather quickly. Our real concern is concussion."

Speaking more like a nurse than a lover, she demonstrated the emotional distance and objectivity we expect of medical practitioners. I instinctively rejected the mask. "You look worried."

"Of course, I'm worried! When I got the call, they didn't know how severely you've been concussed. I'm glad you keep my business card in your wallet. That's how they found me—just arriving at the hospital for work."

"Where am I?"

"Boulder County Hospital. They were able to get you here in less than forty minutes."

I looked again at my bare chest and saw a tube running from a bandage below my armpit into a water bottle contraption. "A punctured lung?"

"Yes, a pneumothorax due to blunt trauma."

"Oh, yes. I remember the handlebar slamming against my chest just before my head connected with the pavement—"

"You could have been killed. Thank God you weren't going faster."

"The truck driver?"

"Uninjured. You took the brunt of the accident."

Pain waved up from my lower left leg through my chest to a dull headache completely encircling my head. "Whose fault?"

"That's unclear. The trucker did an unsafe turn, but the cops think you were speeding. They didn't write a ticket."

I closed my eyes to refocus and consider the newest saga of my accident-filled life. This must be the twenty-sixth or twenty-seventh injury involving hospital treatment. How many broken bones? At least ten or twelve...I had forgotten.

"Jody, see if you can connect with Tom Queen. I want to get on a vitamin C drip as soon as possible. He can set it up at home." Being a fan of Dr. Linus Pauling, the Nobel Prize-winning molecular chemist, I am a great believer in the power of vitamin C to stimulate tissue regeneration and faster healing. Tom, also a devotee, was one of the few chiropractors I knew who could get the intravenous high-dose form of the vitamin.

"You know I don't buy into that therapy."

"Let's not debate this now. You know where I stand."

"You're so obstinate about alternative medical therapies."

"The path to health and well-being has other routes besides through big pharma." Suddenly I smelled musty sweetness and earthy odors of my grandmother's health food store where I had spent many breaks to escape from the brutality and onslaught of military school. She had taught me so much about ancient wisdom and about the medical practices of non-Western cultures. Her store had always attracted an eclectic group of customers in search of natural healing methods, and I had listened to many animated conversations between Grandma and her admiring followers. She had personified a modern-day witch doctor. I guess years of indoctrination changed me forever, predisposing me to serious doubts about Western medicine practices—except for treatment of acute traumatic injuries, my immediate predicament.

"Are you still with us?

"Yes, I'm still here. I was just recalling my grandma's health food store."

"I wish I could have met the grand lady," Jody sighed. She often seemed regretful that she did not have a chance to share in all the chapters of my life before we met. Maybe she felt those experiences would have helped her understand my complex personality.

"What's next?"

"Well, the neurologist will watch you for at least forty-eight hours to make sure your concussion doesn't involve deeper brain trauma. They won't remove the chest tube for two to four days until they are sure that you're not leaking air into your chest cavity. Then you'll be released for home care. You're facing rehab due to that leg injury—"

"Rehab won't be necessary. I can take care of that myself."

"I agree. They know you're an exercise physiologist. But is an attorney wise to represent herself in court? Does a surgeon perform an appendectomy on himself? It's better to have physical therapists involved in your rehab."

"That won't be necessary. I can design my own rehab program. I've done it before."

"Whatever, my love." Concern again appeared with an intense stare and small wrinkles forming around her eyes.

"I appreciate your concern...and you being here when I woke up." I reached for her reassuring hand. "Your presence provides more healing energy than an entire pharmacy."

A thirty-something neurologist marched into the room, clearly pleased to see that I was awake and conversing with Jody. He looked so young and inexperienced. He took a quick look at a chart near the foot of my bed and then spoke to me. "Great to see you are awake and talking with your friend! How do you feel?"

"A little achy and a bit dizzy but ready to go for a run."

"You won't be running for a while...not until your broken leg heals."

Jody addressed the young resident. "You don't know Luke. He'll be running before most people would stop using a cane to assist with balance."

The young doctor smiled, obviously having some fun. "A difficult patient, huh? Why am I not surprised? Any guy who rides a Harley without a helmet is clearly a hard case."

The doctor moved closer and peered into my eyes. With a small flashlight, he ran me through a few tests by asking me to follow the light with my eyes. He then produced a card with various sizes of type and asked me to read a paragraph. He examined my head, palpating the area that had produced a significant goose egg, a hematoma. He rubbed his fingers together near my ears to determine if I could hear the sounds, which I could. He asked me to recall my memory of the accident, which unfortunately was crystal clear, and my recitation of events before the crash was more brutal than I think Jody wanted to hear. He grabbed my tongue with a piece of gauze and pulled it forward while asking me to say "Ahhhh." I must have passed the examination with flying colors. "Well, no significant neurologic damage apparent that I can see, but we need to watch you for the next few hours."

Suddenly, I felt a rush of weariness overtake my pain and then a strong urge to sleep. He must have read my expression.

"We can't let you fall asleep...not yet, not for a few hours. You understand?"

I still felt a bit disoriented, but my medical knowledge was easy to retrieve from memory. "Yes, you need to be sure the concussion isn't more than a hard bump on the head and there are not additional complications such as internal bleeding. Right?"

"The X-rays didn't show any major problems, but we need to make sure. You were out cold for almost two hours. Your friend can keep you occupied until we judge it safe to let you sleep. A few more hours."

"Pain medication?"

"Sorry. You seem like a tough guy, so I need you to tough it out for a few hours. I'll prescribe something that you can begin taking later today. You take care in the meantime." With that, the physician patted my right leg and breezed out of the room.

"Will you get rid of the bike?" Jody pled.

"I can't. You know what you bought here. A risk taker. This isn't going to change because of one minor motorcycle accident."

"A minor accident? Minor? Luke, you could have been killed this morning. Just a few more feet and that truck's rear tire would have rolled over you."

"I may have been close to the edge. But I was living at full throttle. You know how it is. I'll be more cautious in the future. Maybe a helmet—"

"Do I need a witness? Where is that nurse?"

"I hate to make you worry about my safety all the time. But that's who I am: a risk taker. It's not only the way I choose to live but it's also my work. I'm so damn tired. I got up early this morning. Okay, a helmet."

She dropped the professional veneer and placed her head on my right shoulder. I loved her so much at that moment. I stroked her soft hair and recited a silent prayer to my higher power who had saved me again. That day was *not* a good day to die. Jody deserved better results: enhanced preparation, more caution next time. Let it flow.

Chapter 5

SCHOOL

*Fall 1956, St. Mark's Military School,
near Estes Park, Colorado*

I detested that place. They called it military school, but it felt more like a prison during many days. I had been stuck there for over three years. Several years had passed since a surgeon removed the tumor and some of my neck and shoulder muscles, and I had become weary of incessant teasing about the dent in my neck. That was not funny anymore; it had never been amusing. It had been their fault for allowing the cancer to grow so large before surgeons in Kansas City excised it. The brainless school doctor had told me not to worry—just an insignificant, benign bump that would soon fade away. He was an imbecile! After his misguided pronouncement and the devastating aftermath, he wouldn't even acknowledge me when I passed him on the quad.

I attempted to make the best of that bizarre and glum asylum. Some aspects were okay. I appreciated the military themes: reveille in the morning and taps in the evening and our parade formations and marches. Those rituals made me feel part of something important, as if we were recruits in the real Marines. Some kids were okay and tolerable; some were delinquents and nut jobs and budding perverts.

My two roommates became my salvation. School authorities had classified Danny and Sammy as "troubled kids" like me, but I never witnessed any major behavioral issues that became alarming. Sammy had a short fuse and could become angry without provocation, and Danny could be difficult to communicate with following his dad's irregular visitations.

I knew how he felt because my mom's occasional visits inspired melancholy. She was doing great in Las Vegas where she worked as an entertainer. My school's adult officers appreciated her visits because they thought she was a fox, as one of them had brazenly informed me with wink-heavy allusions. She looked so beautiful and happy and often told me she felt regret that I had to be there, but she had to look after my bizarre big sister who still lived with her. Joanne caused enough trouble, she said. Mom didn't have time to raise me properly, and I had been running around with some juvenile delinquents—getting into skirmishes with neighborhood bullies. She promised that I could fly to Las Vegas and stay with her and watch her sing and dance. She had been saying that for a while, but I knew this promise, while well intended, wasn't true. During holidays and summer breaks, I always returned to my grandmother's herb-infused home in Kansas City, and sometimes I didn't see Mom at all during those long, humid summers. That's why I became sad when she departed following her stopovers, a raw kind of nothing-left feeling. I became wary that someday she might stop visiting. I wouldn't have blamed her if she had.

To inspire some happy interludes, my roommates and I played board games when we were not studying. We played

Monopoly a lot—that was my favorite—Sammy's too. Danny won most of the time, but he didn't care if he won or lost. I found that uncanny because who doesn't like to win Monopoly? We also played *Battleship*, *Clue*, and, when we could get our hands on it, *The Game of Life*. When that game proposed a choice of money, power, or fame, I always defaulted to fame. Even during my emerging adolescence, I knew I had a message to convey, and fame could become a soapbox.

The school was similar in layout to a small college campus with old brick-and-stone buildings surrounding an immense yard called the quad. Adjacent to the buildings, a running track encircled a football field, also used for soccer. I jogged around the old cinder track as much as I could. Mountains rose all around us, but we didn't journey to the Outpost much, a camping area where they staged chuck wagon barbecues and campfire sing-a-longs. I would have hiked up there all the time, but they only allowed us to go once in the early fall and again just before summer recess. They said it got too cold up there most other times during the school year.

Some of the upperclassmen were jerks. They thought of themselves as cool dudes. I tried to stay away from them as much as I could, but we couldn't avoid them at the mess hall. The older guys had a prescribed gathering area, and younger plebes had another area. They strictly enforced segregation. One miserable jerk incessantly teased Danny, but his self-important wit was never amusing. Danny hated him.

The worst of the bunch was a control freak they called Sarge—Sarge Deville. He was a drill sergeant and had been at the school for almost five years. I recall that his actual first name was Sylvester, which became fodder for laughter during private conversations among plebes. He planned to graduate at the end of that school year. Good riddance, I often announced to my roommates. He had clobbered a few kids with impunity. He threatened to beat me up on several occasions because I had refused to be compliant in his presence. He would brownnose the commanding officers, and they let him do pretty much what he wanted to do; he thought he owned the school. He often became our drill sergeant, and we could tell he craved authority. As if pinching his nose, he barked at us with an intimidating accent. I never saw him smile, and he had mastered a signature "evil eye." He was bad news, and Danny and Sammy and I stayed away from him as much as we could.

Something huge happened about halfway through the fall semester of that year. Sammy ran into our room one day and asked us to cross-your-hearts-and-hope-to-die if he told us a secret. We crossed and hoped as requested, and so he told us to follow him. We snuck outside into a dark, moonless night. Sammy kept us close to B-barracks where we lived and then we dashed behind the science building. Realizing this wasn't such a great idea, I became apprehensive, considering the consequences. But we followed Sammy around a garage where the school stored snowplows, lawn mowers, and yard equipment. Behind the garage were four or five car-sized boulders. Among these rocks, we came upon a stray mother dog—quite dead. But she had birthed three puppies, and they weren't dead—they were squirmy and whiny.

Sammy announced that we could each have a puppy. They weren't his to bestow as gifts, but nobody owned them either. Their momma dog indeed was lifeless, so we hatched a rescue plan. There was a long and narrow closet in our room where we kept clothes. At the back of that closet, we had discovered a trapdoor and behind the door, an empty space with nothing but a few bent curtain rods and a nonfunctioning lamp. I assumed they had used it for storage before we came along, but they had forgotten about the hidden room because they would have locked it up. Sammy's steamer trunk covered the door, and thus we transformed the clandestine room into our clubhouse.

So, we each grabbed a puppy—mine was brown with white spots—and took them back to our room. We were lucky that night because nobody saw us sneak into the barracks. We created a nest in the clubhouse from one of our extra wool blankets. Danny scurried to a snack room where cadets could buy beverages and sundries. He returned with three cartons of milk. We could tell the puppies were famished because they drank all the milk within a few moments. One of them pooped on some newspapers that we had placed on the floor, and we agreed to take turns cleaning up often because we couldn't let our closet smell like dog poop. That would have gotten us busted pronto and would have also guaranteed detention.

None of us had ever owned a dog before. I don't believe I had ever seen Danny so joyful. I know in time his puppy could have helped him deal with his ever-present sadness. We played with them every night before bedtime, a sublime distraction from harsh, lonely days. Those puppies had helped us feel better about being inmates of St. Mark's.

Several weeks after adopting the puppies, loud whimpering woke me just before dawn. One of the puppies—I think

Sammy's—missed his momma a lot. We had become accustomed to occasional yips and whines, but this sounded more like canine screams. "Hey, Sammy...Larry is whining. We'll get caught."

We had named the puppies after the three stooges: Larry, Curley, and Moe. Larry was Sammy's puppy. Danny adopted Curley—because his puppy was the fattest like Curley, the portly human character from the movies. And we named my puppy Moe because he was bossiest. Sammy called Moe the alpha dog—leader of the pack.

"Hey, Sammy, wake up! Larry is going to get us in trouble." Sammy must have stayed up late playing with the puppies like he often did. But then he sometimes wouldn't wake up and get dressed following reveille. He had already been in trouble twice that fall for not getting to morning formation on time. "Sammy!"

"Huh?"

"It's Larry. He's whining too loudly. You've got to shut him up! He's almost screaming!"

Danny added, "Yeah, Sammy. Get up and pet him or something. You're the only one who can calm him down."

Sammy rolled over and sat up on the edge of his bed. "Something's wrong with him. I think he's sick. He whined a lot last night, but I couldn't keep my eyes open any longer." We could hear Larry getting louder and louder. Sammy shuffled to the closet and opened the hidden door. I had never heard a dog whine so loudly before this—it was frightening.

Someone beat on our room door. Oh, God! We were busted. Danny and I didn't move, just glaring at each other. Bam! Bam! Bam! "Open the door now!" It was a mature upper classman's voice—Sarge Deville. We had also locked our door in violation of the rules.

"Sammy," I whispered. "Get inside the clubhouse and shut the door." I stood and stepped into my trousers. No way I was going to answer the door in just my skivvies. I opened the door to see Sarge Deville flanked by two upperclassmen. They had been alerted by other kids rooming near us.

"What's going on in here?" barked Sarge.

"One of us had a bad dream."

Danny said, "Yeah, it was me, Sarge. I was having a nightmare and shouting."

The stern idiot barged into our room without an invitation. "That didn't sound like some stupid kid screaming, did it?" Another upperclassman shook his head negatively.

Sarge began inspecting our room, peeking under our beds and pushing chairs away from our study desks. "Where's that other roommate of yours...that kid, Samuel Harris?"

I glanced at Danny and he shrugged his shoulders. "We just woke up, Sarge. Who knows?"

Then everyone heard loud, pitiful whining. Sarge jumped into our closest, pushing our hanging clothes around. He found the secret trapdoor behind Sammy's trunk, jerked it open, and discovered Sammy with the dogs and Larry in his lap. Moe dashed out of the clubhouse ready to play. "What's this shit! Dogs are against every regulation we have at St. Mark's. Get out of there and bring that other puppy."

Sammy crawled out of the clubhouse with a puppy in each hand. Larry continued to whine with a piercing screech. Moe trotted over to me and I picked him up. He chewed my fingers, ready to play.

Sarge displayed his evil eye at Danny. "Take that goddamn pillowcase off your pillow and give it to me! Now!"

Danny handed over a pillowcase. I could see his hands shaking. I was not shaking about anything. That damned asshole.

"Give me those puppies," he said to Sammy.

I refused to put up with this crap. "No! They're our puppies and we're taking care of them until they're big enough for adoption."

"I'm going to kick your stupid ass if you don't obey orders. Now!"

Sammy said, "Let's obey orders, Lukey." He handed Curley to Sarge. The jerk dropped the puppy into a pillowcase.

"The other dog," Sarge ordered. Sammy handed over Larry, still whimpering. We needed to get that dog to a vet. He was sick and in danger.

I said, "The puppy needs to go to a vet. He's sick. They shouldn't be put in a pillowcase together like that."

"You...plebe! Follow the Sarge's orders," barked another upperclassman.

Other kids in the barracks gathered outside our door. Everyone was looking at me. I petted Moe a couple of times and handed him to Sarge. The bastard dropped my puppy into the pillowcase. I pleaded for mercy. "Moe, it's okay!"

"Get dressed this minute, all three of you." Sarge and the other upperclassmen stared at us while we put on our uniforms. All three dogs barked and whined and squirmed within the dangling pillowcase. Who could blame them? The kids who had gathered outside our room chattered and laughed as if this was an impromptu hazing party, an entertaining sideshow. After we dressed, Sarge said, "Follow me." He then gave orders to one of the older guys. "Get me a rope and the baseball bat leaning behind the door in my room."

"Yes, sir." The guy scooted out of our room.

We followed behind Sarge and the other upperclassman through the corridor of the barracks and then outside. There must have been twenty-five kids following us. It was still dark and frosty. Mountain air smelled invigorating at that time of morning, and I considered running into the mountains where they would never find me again.

I couldn't stand this abuse of authority. "What are you going to do with our puppies?"

Sarge didn't look back at me. "I think you've been here for two or three years and you still don't understand who is boss. Rules are rules. That's the point of all your training. And you just don't get it, do you?"

"I have never seen any rules about rescuing puppies from their dead momma. The Humane Society would call us heroes!" Danny started crying as if a toddler. I understood then that he'd be miserable for a long time after this.

The fetching upperclassman trotted back to us with a baseball bat and rope. Sarge stopped below one of the gigantic blue spruces growing near our barracks. I loved those trees, especially when they were shrouded with fluffy new snow. Larry, Curley, and Moe whined and barked, an oppressive assault in the early morning solitude.

Sarge tied one end of the rope to the pillowcase and threw the other end over a branch several feet above his head. He then fixed the rope to the tree trunk.

I shouted, "No! You can't do that! That's cruelty to animals. It's against the law!"

Sarge projected his evil eye with a shitty smile. Our peers appeared stupefied, unwilling to protest or react. He stepped back as if at home plate. "Cruelty to animals, you say? They won't feel a thing, I promise." Then he whacked the bag as if swinging for a homerun. I'm sure Moe shrieked and screamed. I knew his bark as if he had been my child. Sarge swung the bat five more times, and then two more times, and the pillowcase became blood-drenched and silent.

"Now you guys are going to dig a hole behind the barracks at the edge of the forest and bury those dogs." He looked at Sammy and added, "And you...you hang on to the pillowcase. Wash it by hand if you want, but you're not sending it to the laundry. Then you're going to put it on your pillow and sleep on it tonight. That's your punishment for hiding yourself and those dogs in that goddamn closet crawlspace."

I could not hold my rage in check any longer. "You are an asshole, Sarge...*a fucking asshole!*"

The drill sergeant sprinted over to me, grabbed my jacket, and lifted me up on my tiptoes. "And you...you seem to have problems adjusting here. I can help you clarify priorities. Now you're in charge of cleaning the heads in the upperclassman's barracks. All of them. Every day. You'll do it after taps, before you study or go to sleep. And, by God, that puppy pillowcase is on your bed from now till I'm gone from this lunatic asylum next spring."

I swung a clenched fist at his jaw, but he blocked my arm and threw me to the ground. "Cleaning our shitters is perfect punishment for a crooked head like you."

I jumped up and rushed at him, swinging my fists in wide circles. "You're a murderer. Everyone knows you're a criminal!"

He threw me to the ground again and stepped on my chest. "Get up again and I'll put your lights out." Nobody rushed forward to intercede. The entire group of plebe spectators could have taken him down, but they were afraid of the big tormenter and his sycophants. I had been subdued by his superior strength and body mass, but I would never let him diminish my righteous indignation.

And so, I slept with my crooked head on that pillowcase every night from then on, even after Sarge departed at the end of that school year. As I drifted off to sleep, I would often remember the squirmy stooges who had given my roommates and me some of our happiest moments together at St. Mark's Military School for Boys.

Fall 1996, University of Denver

I gazed across a sea of faces in the Driscoll Student Center at the University of Denver. Most of the students were natural science or social science majors. They looked younger than I thought we looked when I was an undergraduate. A few had unambiguous expressions of curiosity, not amusement. They knew my reputation, and some were aspiring health and fitness devotees. Cognitive neuroscience, biochemistry, sociology, gender studies…a rich variety of college majors were covered by this group of students and professors. A few were looking for pearls; others were just there for entertainment from an exercise physiologist and sports psychologist who had leapt off a bridge in the name of science.

"About a third of you have too much body fat," I started. "Most of you are sedentary by historical standards, wired as you are to your laptops and video games. Some of you smoke cigarettes and other noxious weed—"

My obvious reference to cannabis hit the right note as they laughed. "Almost all of you have grown up on a diet dominated by sugar, salt, hydrogenated fats, and chemicals with names too tortuous to pronounce. I'm talking about McDonald's here, folks." Laughter again filled the lecture hall.

"We're all victims of the technologies our species invented to manage the dangers of the natural environment. Those technologies can certainly kill us before our time if we allow ourselves to be lured into complacency.

"When we substitute pickles for spinach, catsup candy for real tomato sauce, and corn-fattened beef for plant-based sources of protein, we're setting up future consequences. Those consequences can include cardiovascular disease, Type II diabetes, metabolic syndrome, cancer, and, yes, the most feared of all aging diseases: dementia.

"And the decisions you're making today—what you eat, how much you exercise, how long you sleep, how well you manage the stress of college life, how frequently you socialize with other humans—these choices are influencing the quality of life and vitality that an old man or woman in the future will have or not have. Are you willing to apologize to the older you for failing to take care of yourself now? Or are you willing to send your future self a better message about the legacy of vigor you are creating today?

"That conversation with your aged self might go something like this: 'I did my best to protect and preserve my vitality and health so you, older me, can live each day with abundant energy and continuing engagement, a life worth living long after the bloom of youth has fallen away. You don't have to be a passenger in life's journey just because you're old now. I've made sure you are still a driver.'"

I stopped and engaged my audience with intense eye contact. They understood then that I meant business, and only a few continued sitting there with cynical body posture, perhaps thinking that I was just a nut job. I clicked a USB slide changer connected to my laptop, and the screen transformed from black to a photo of me in midair, obviously depicting the fateful first moments of my jump off the Paseo Bridge.

"An easy, protected, sedentary way of life does not prepare you for the other end of your time on planet earth because you won't learn how to handle adversity. The more battles you create for yourself—when you truly confront the essence of who you are as a person with unknown potential—the more you will know that challenges prepare you for life after fifty or sixty and beyond. And we know now, more than we've ever known before, that the second half of life can be even richer and more fulfilling than what can be attained in the first half. If you're going to meet your destiny in control, rather than be controlled by it, then you must commit to becoming a warrior."

The next slide depicted Jody and me underwater in a swimming pool wearing our scuba outfits, each grabbing the other's private parts as if beginning foreplay. Laughter crisscrossed the room.

"The belief that old age is out of our control is just that: a myth. Advances in neuroscience, molecular biology, and social psychology are convincing today's enlightened thinkers on active aging that we can stay in the driver's seat for most of our advanced old age. We can expand our own productive longevity.

"The nonnegotiable physical changes of aging, long assumed to be genetically predestined, are myths. Increased body fat, increased blood pressure, decreased bone density, loss of flexibility and strength—these changes are not necessarily a function of the aging process. Morbidity takes us down more because of poor lifestyle choices and unhealthy practices than because of the aging process."

I wandered from one side of the stage to the other, again staring intently from one audience member to another, making sure that each person felt that my message was personal and specific. "You become your decisions and choices. None are completely insignificant, even choosing a soy burger over a Big Mac for lunch today. Some decisions are so consequential that they can change your life forever. The guiding principle of my relationship to food is simple: 'I eat to live; I don't live to eat.'"

Sitting in the fourth row next to the middle aisle, a twenty-something graduate student, sporting a goatee and shoulder-length hair, raised his hand and waved it when I didn't immediately acknowledge him. I finally called on him by pointing.

He said, "This is all theoretical mishmash, but I'm not hearing anything that gives me an understanding of your sense of urgency. What's supposed to make this real for us? Most of us are in our twenties!"

"Then let me tell you a story about a consequential decision that changed a life." As if the question had been posed by a clack, I switched the slide again to show me running side-by-side with another man, shorter and leaner and younger than me.

"I was in graduate school at the University of Kansas, as you know, pursuing double PhD degrees in exercise physiology and sports psychology. Not only was I pursuing these degrees, I was somewhat of a rarity because I was as athletically fit as you see in this photo. It was ironic that many of my student peers and a lot of the professors were in a lot worse condition than me. Most didn't practice what they learned and preached.

"I was dating an associate professor in the psych department, and one day I stopped by her condo unannounced. She was entertaining several of her graduate students to get to know them better before the fall semester really got started.

"One young student wanted to talk with me a little more intensely than I was prepared to oblige. Let me be frank: I visited Marsha with lovemaking on my mind, not deep intellectual discussions with insecure grad students." My audience chuckled again.

"During this conversation with Gordon, he confessed that he was having great difficulty trying to kick cigarettes. He had definite reasons to be concerned—in addition to the fact that he was at that time smoking a pack or two of cigarettes per day.

"Let me put this in perspective. This was the early 1970s, and the tobacco industry was thriving. Around 50 percent of all adult men in the United States smoked cigarettes, the twentieth century symbol of rebellious culture, the rise of Marlboro Man.

"Hollywood icons such as Sammy Davis Jr., Yul Brynner, George Peppard, and Steve McQueen popularized the habit. I'm sure you're familiar with some, if not all, of these famous names—all of whom eventually died from smoking-related diseases. Most of you have probably seen TV shows from the fifties and sixties with news personalities and celebrities smoking as they worked. A monolithic tobacco industry employed marketing trickery to make the dangerous habit appear benign if not downright healthful. Smoking was a cultural norm celebrated in marketing and movies.

"Gordon had become hooked on cigarettes around the time when the United States Surgeon General announced that cigarette smoking might be the cause of lung cancer and other serious diseases. By the time he became a graduate student, he was smoking almost nonstop throughout the day, and lung abuse was taking a toll on his health. Even in his early twenties he could feel his health declining with smoker's cough and decreased lung capacity."

I hesitated for a moment to study the photo filling the screen behind me. "By the early seventies, the connections between smoking and cancer were gaining wider acceptance despite extraordinary denials by tobacco companies. Gordon knew his long-term health was on the line, especially since—and here's an amazing detail—he grew up with asthma and almost died during one severe attack at age four. After being rushed to the hospital by ambulance, he was then hospitalized for a couple of weeks because of lung disease, and he could still remember the terrors of hospitalization and being confined inside an oxygen tent.

"Isn't it astonishing that someone who had such profound encounters with lung disease nevertheless became hooked by an industry that had perfected the art of marketing to teenagers?" I paused again for dramatic effect and could see that almost every person in the room was thinking about the personal implications of what I was saying.

"I knew that Gordon didn't want to hear a lecture. He already understood the slippery slope he was then sliding down. So, I invited him to go jogging with me the following Saturday. He had been jogging recreationally even though he smoked, so he wasn't totally out of shape. Hesitant at first, he finally accepted my invitation once I reassured him that this was not going to be a competitive race or anything like that—just a recreational run in a park on a beautiful fall day.

"We ran in Broken Arrow Park in Lawrence near Haskell Indian Nations University, and at first he kept pace with me, being young and lean. But as the miles stretched out my proficient stride left him trailing behind. I didn't try to race him or intimidate him with my greater fitness; I demonstrated the value of a healthy body. I was just running my normal pace.

"I think he was impressed with how effortlessly I could run and my superior stamina. What's the old cliché attributed to Buddha? *When the student is ready, the teacher will appear?*

"Because health was what Gordon wanted more than anything after a childhood of chronic illness, he quit smoking cold turkey four days later, his twenty-fourth birthday. This wasn't his first attempt at quitting but probably his tenth. I never scolded or lectured him about smoking but caused him to seek health because of the example I set and the possibilities that true fitness can endow. I put the lifestyle choices in front of him. He made the choice of healthy living and longevity."

Wandering across the stage, I folded up my arms and looked again at the photo. "You can see how he looks, how fit. My girlfriend took this photo just two years ago, so it's been almost twenty-five years since I met Gordon and we became friends. I believe he looks younger than his real age. His most recent annual physical, which included a treadmill stress test, concluded that today he is in excellent cardiovascular health. He hasn't had a severe asthma attack since he quit smoking. He is a living testament to the power of will over bad habits. And, by the way, if it isn't obvious to you yet, when I met Gordon he was in the age range that most of you are in now."

I looked again at the student who had asked me the challenging question. "If he were here in this lecture hall today, Gordon would be quick to assure you that he owes his health to a chance encounter with me. Or maybe it wasn't a chance encounter. He discovered in me another man who also had childhood battles with disease, including lots of infections and cancer, someone who has embraced a way of life today that overcomes our human tendencies to fall into decline as we grow older. We are brothers on this journey together toward a future we control, one that does not control us.

"Whether you like it or not, try to believe me that your life is a battle. It's a battle of choices. It's a battle of adversities that you must overcome to thrive. It's a battle against aging. Those of you who will grab spears and face the world as fighters are the warriors who will survive long into a robust and purposeful old age."

Applause so generous uplifted me following an impassioned lecture to those university students and faculty. And in my mind's eye, I saw once again an eleven-year-old boy who had become determined one bitter night—in an hour of screaming darkness when his puppy had been beaten to death by a psychopath—that he would get in shape and stay that way. Never again would someone beat anything or anyone he loved. *Never*.

Chapter 6

PATIENT

Fall 1993, Denver, Colorado

"I can't."

"Luke, you must get it checked out." Jody pushed up on her left elbow and looked at me with imploring blue eyes that have called me to attention many times.

"You don't understand. I can't."

"Yes, my love, you can. I'll take you myself."

I threw off the sheets and willed myself to get out of bed. I dropped to the floor and in less than thirty seconds I ripped off fifty pushups with Jody respecting my ritual without interruption. She had finally accepted my tendencies to the use the world as my gymnasium. Push-ups here; wall squats over there; stair runs everywhere. "I'm okay. I promise."

"Now you're speaking like a child in denial."

"It's been close to forty years. Everything should be fine. I've never had more energy." I wandered around the expansive master bedroom feeling observed and caged. She had trapped me in more ways than one.

"I'm proud of you." Jody threw back the sheets from her naked body, lissome, tan, and muscular. Morning light fell through leaded-glass windows and illuminated her skin in patchworks with beautiful rainbow streaks illustrating her skin. "Did you hear me, Luke? I said I'm proud of you."

I glared in an antique mirror above my chest of drawers and saw her standing behind me, so sensual and perfect, a middle-aged woman at the peak of her sexuality. God, I'm a lucky man, but I often wished that men and women would reach their sexual crescendos at the same developmental moments. I still felt horny but not nearly as ravenous as I had been during my late teens and early twenties. "Thank you, my sweetheart. I'm proud of you also." I turned to face her, breasts firm, hips in perfect proportion to her chest. I admired her legs more than any other feature of her anatomy—runner's legs, neither too muscular nor too skinny. Long, strong, and proportioned.

"Damn it. Will you stop it?"

"Huh?"

"Stop checking me out and pay attention. You do this all the time. Sometimes I think you have ADD, attention deficit disorder."

"Honey, I am paying attention. I hear you. You want me to get the lump examined. I just can't face another carousel of tests. I think I'm fine. Nothing to be concerned about."

She sauntered over and wrapped her arms around my waist, yawning and still sleepy after a previous night of too much chardonnay and a lot of screwing. "We shouldn't even need to have this discussion. You're an exercise physiologist. You know your body as well as a watchmaker understands a finely tuned watch. You recognize something's probably wrong."

"I've told you this before: My body tends to throw off tumors. They've always been benign. A dozen or more of them over the decades. I've stopped allowing fear to control me every time a bump appears somewhere on my body." I glanced away from our embrace to see my reflection in the mirror. I could see that the area around my Adam's apple was larger than normal. It had been that way for months, and it seemed to be enlarging.

She looked at me with a pleading expression, and her wide bedroom eyes displayed a ferocity that had kept me interested longer than has any other woman in my past. "I won't take 'no' or 'can't' for an answer any longer. Make an appointment or I will. Right now! Today."

I kissed her full, pouty lips, sensing again our special connection that made me feel so accepted. I placed my hand gently on her right breast and fondled her nipple between my thumb and forefinger. She started to moan and snuggle closer but then pushed back. "Let's not get distracted right now," she said with encouragement rather than rejection in her tone. "You can have your way with me after your appointment with an oncologist."

"That could take days or even weeks! How about after I *schedule* an appointment?"

She smiled and shook my awakening cock as if making a deal with an old friend. "Compromise accepted."

With a great deal of forbearance, I turned away from Jody and reached for the Yellow Pages below the phone next to my bed, and I thumbed through the pages until I found listings for medical doctors specializing in oncology. My penis returned to flaccid.

Dr. Sen was a storied physician with a well-known reputation in my clinical network. His medical receptionist gave me a couple of appointment alternatives, one for Friday, just three days from then—a cancelled appointment, lucky me—and another option for three weeks later. Jody had left our bedroom to make coffee in the kitchen, but I defeated temptation to make the appointment further out and agreed to see Sen the following Friday. I deserved major sexual gratification for this. She would be proud of me. On my breakfast menu for this day would be a blow job followed by long and lingering cunnilingus. Coffee and croissants optional.

Luke doesn't grasp how much I hate him since he hasn't seen me in years. I've been quiet these last four decades, but I've been around. I'm good at guerrilla warfare, with being inconspicuous my specialty. Not a single medical test had discovered me in my hiding places deep inside a few cells in that miraculous gland they call the "thyroid." I've been most patient; you've got to give me that.

The astonishing irony is that he hasn't stopped thinking about me, not ever. Weeks, sometimes months pass when he seems to forget his enemy. He gets wrapped up in books and work and women. But then he'll be having dinner somewhere late at night, and he'll glance up and see his reflection in a street-facing window. He'll notice a slight tilt to his head, the absence of muscles in his otherwise well-proportioned neck. Then he'll recall mummy boy, the terror of losing so much at such a young age. You'd think forty years would be enough to eliminate his lingering anxieties of recurrence, the delirious freedom of denial, but that's the cool thing about mean Mr. Cancer: always there somewhere, in mind, body, or both.

He remembers they told him that "cure" and "cancer" are not compatible words and that he'll always be at risk for recurrence, though the probabilities diminish with time; and they believed they had excised the entire tumor and surrounding diseased tissue. They took enough healthy tissue away at the margins. For that he was slightly disfigured for life. Recall: this is a good thing in the story of this boy growing up. I became the foundation for his motivations and tenacity. I became his archenemy. So, he became almost superhumanly determined to hide his cosmetic flaws with weight lifting, aerobics, and competitive sports. Humans are miraculously self-delusional. *Hope springs eternal*, said Alexander Pope, a long-dead poet from that self-deluding species who, predictably, lost all hope and found finality.

So here I am again, growing like a weed in this warm, wet, and wonderful tissue. I like my new home a lot. It's a gland located just below Luke's Adam's apple, kind of shaped like a butterfly. He has a prominent Adam's apple naturally, which has made him look more masculine and stronger. Now his Adam's apple area is starting to look scary.

Just for your edification, his thyroid, like yours, makes and stores hormones that help regulate heart rate, blood pressure, body temperature, and the velocity at which food can be converted into energy. Thyroid hormones pretty much run the show and impact performance of every cell in the human body. Tiny gland, big job.

In a few words, because cancer never likes to be boring, if your thyroid isn't working right, you know there's a problem brewing. Luke has known for weeks. He's totally tuned into his body. The swelling is a no-brainer, but he's been quick to rationalize that. He also has had some trouble swallowing, and, considering all the vegetables he chomps on every day, difficulty swallowing has been a noticeable inconvenience. It's tough to enjoy broccoli when you feel like you're swallowing jagged rocks. He's also been clearing his throat a lot. That woman he sleeps with has noticed; he's wakened her several times, and she's stayed awake the rest of the night fretting over what the heck's going on.

Luke has had some night sweats, and a few times he's been cold on a warm, sunny day. So, his body temperature has been screwed up. Oops. He is proud of his mane of dark, wavy hair, almost Samson-like, and he's noticed more hair than usual on his hairbrush and the shower floor.

This guy won't take sitting down as a solution to anything even though of late he has been tired after a normal business day helping his cardiac patients recover from bypass surgeries. His overdeveloped heart muscle—one of his proudest achievements, believe it or not—has been beating somewhat irregularly, and he's noticed a few palpitations, especially when he runs wind sprints. He's felt like retiring to bed early some evenings, and that lack of vitality has bothered him most. Normally his energy level has no typical boundaries.

Put simply: the great regulator of Luke's body and mind has gone haywire, and he can thank yours truly.

That Indian doctor didn't mess around. After taking Luke's history and learning of his overexposure to X-ray radiation as an infant, and then his sarcoma in childhood, the doctor ordered a needle biopsy. That event triggered my certitude that I was going to be a short-timer, at least this incarnation of me. I made myself too obvious, but I had bet on ignorance and complacency. Only about 5 percent of lumps around the thyroid are cancerous, so not to worry. But Luke's medical history left little doubt to the physician: his enemy had returned. The test proved positive.

Luke, being Luke, took control of the gloomy turn of events. He started getting in even better shape. He ran five, ten, or more miles every day. He lifted weights. He endured several intravenous infusions in his veins with a liquid containing twenty-five grams of vitamin C and a buffer to keep his blood from becoming too acidic. He wished to believe—and there are others like him—that this vitamin can play a role in deterring cancerous cell growth. What fools they are with their potions and machines! He ate handfuls of vitamins and meditated, imagining what I look like and then attacking me with his white blood cells. I've noticed more blood supply building up around me, but those nuisance white cells haven't accomplished anything. I thrived, I grew, I conquered.

So, one day they excised me and my new home from Luke's neck. I'm not entirely unhappy about that because, like I told you, I know I'm mortal just like my host but I'm goal-driven. My realistic and attainable objective is to win before the end. Cut me out today: that's a battle I lose today. But I'm a fighter who's intrepid and persistent. There will be more battles to come, and I intend to win before the end: the last tissue standing.

My neck needed to remain wrapped. The wound still oozed, so the white gauze had a few brownish stains. People glanced and hesitated when they passed me in the grocery store. It had been two days since Dr. Sen and his surgical team removed my thyroid gland, a total thyroidectomy. I had stayed in the hospital overnight but recovered quickly from the anesthesia. Other than a little hoarseness and mild neck pain around the site of the two-inch incision, I felt fine. His nurse had given me a list of postoperative instructions that filled four typed pages, single-spaced. After cautioning me about infection and what to look for should the incision area become infected—as if I wouldn't know—the next important instruction was for me to get plenty of rest. As if I wouldn't know.

That's where Dr. Sen and I parted postoperative philosophies. "Rest" is not in my vocabulary. Jody had tried to play the good nurse by making some incredible chicken-and-rice soup and renting a few James Bond movies from Blockbuster. She knew I had watched those movies many times but that I also sometimes needed to turn off the internal dialogue like everyone does and watch my favorite action hero be *Bond, James Bond*.

She started working soon after my surgery even though she wanted to stay home and mother me. This was part of her maternal instincts, I guess, and she did deserve some time off, but they were shorthanded at the hospital and needed her services. She had left that morning in a rush but not before leaving a pan full of hot Cream of Wheat cereal on the stove with a yellow Post-It note on the counter: "I love you, Luke, and have a great (restful) day, Love J."

I wore the skimpy nylon running shorts she teased me about, my Parris Island Marines T-shirt, and a new pair of Nike running shoes, again a gift from the once-small Seattle shoemaker, which had become a global giant. I stretched as completely as I know how, avoiding lowering my head below my waist. The stitches could have broken and then I'd have been up *shit creek without a paddle*. Harley, my eager, athletic Labrador Retriever was whining to run out the front door to dog freedom. He never ran more than twenty-five yards away from me, nose attached to the ground most of the time, frequent territory-marking tinkle breaks along the way.

Once outside, his master began a slow trot barely faster than walking. We slow-jogged for a couple of blocks to City Park, a special running place for me because it affords a spectacular view of the Denver skyline and Rocky Mountains to the west. The crisp early fall air energized me, and before being fully aware of it, I started running at almost my normal pace. My body turned loose from the shackles of testing, anesthesia, and surgery, feeling free like Harley. I knew then that I was pushing against reality—that I should follow doctor's orders and stay on the couch at home—but there is nothing that makes me feel as whole as recreational running.

A couple of other male runners approached me going the opposite direction, glancing at and wondering about my bandages. I waved at them enthusiastically as they passed, and, as if members of the same fraternal brotherhood, they returned my waves with matching enthusiasm. They knew why I was out there even if I shouldn't have been out there. Glancing at my runner's watch I saw that I had covered five kilometers in thirty-five minutes. Not bad for forty-eight hours post-op. All my preparation and training before surgery had paid off: my reentry flight was a perfect three-point touchdown. I dashed back feeling in the groove.

Harley and I ambled back to my house at a slow walking pace. I must have even worn out the frenetic hunting dog because he followed a step our two behind me without a lot of circling and sniffing. Or maybe he sensed that his master had been injured—

something was in the air—and he chose to stay closer this day, more vigilant about my well-being. I loved that dog. He was a tenacious runner like me.

Upon opening the front door, I shouted into the house, "Hello, I'm back." Jody's car was on the driveway, so I knew she had come for a visit and dinner as promised. She slept with me more nights than not but still had her own apartment. Our arrangement after almost ten years of monogamy still called for separate homes, but we understood that in many ways we were a fully committed couple. My two ex-wives and the two girls I had fathered had made me reluctant to tie the knot again. Maybe I'm not the type of guy to become fully committed to one relationship for life, but I had come to count on Jody's easy and consistent presence.

She appeared from my kitchen. "Where the hell have you been?"

Did I mention *easy and consistent presence*? There was nothing easy about her expression in that moment. I had been busted. Nodding at Harley I began, "We just took an undemanding run. He needs his exercise. This breed requires tons of exercise."

"You know that I would take Harley for a run any day. That excuse is not going to work." She came closer to me and inspected my neck bandages. "You look like you've bled some. I hope you haven't torn the stitches."

"I've been hyperaware of my situation, trust me, honey."

"Don't you even think about 'honeying' me! I don't need to verbalize what I'm thinking right now. You can fill in the blanks."

"Look...Jody...I just needed to run...okay? I felt cooped up. I've watched all the James Bond movies. Watching 007 made me want to run more than ever."

"My mistake. I should have rented movies without so much action. Action heroes like Bond just rev you up."

"Don't blame yourself for anything, hon—Jody. I'm fine! I feel terrific, actually."

She pulled me by the T-shirt into the living room, grabbed my shoulders and shoved me into my favorite recliner. My normal reaction would have been to resist being physically manhandled by such a gorgeous hunk of femininity, but I felt slightly guilty and a bit tuckered out. She had a point. "Okay. We can't subtract your run from your life today, but I don't want you to do this again until Dr. Sen clears you for light physical exercise. I imagine you're probably foolish enough to also start lifting weights. So, your workout room is absolutely off limits. Get it?"

"Sit down, honey. I've made a decision."

Jody settled into an antique dining room chair that I had inherited from my grandmother, her knees together with her hands on her knees, a tense nonverbal message that I had better not mess with her head. "Tell me that you've decided to convalesce like normal postoperative patients. You're going to take it easy, eat the wholesome meals that I'm going to fix you, and, when the moment's right, you're going to fuck my brains out."

I don't laugh a lot being kind of a serious intellectual-jock-fitness-pioneer, but she got me on that one. I laughed so hard that my throat felt like someone had forced me to swallow acid.

"Honey, are you okay?" she asked.

"I'm fine. I've just got to manage myself better when you offer me a fuck." We both giggled, and she finally loosened up her body language, making me feel less like a bad boy and more like the bad man of her dreams.

"You were saying something about a decision?"

"Oh, yes. All this sex talk has distracted me from my mission."

"And that is?"

"Well, you know I've always feared heights more than anything else."

"Yes?"

"While Harley and I were tearing up City Park...I mean jogging casually...I saw this image in my mind of a perfect landing. You know, when an airplane touches down on the tarmac and three wheels kiss the runway without even the slightest hint of a bump."

"I understand the metaphor, but how does it relate to you, Dr. Luke?" I know this way of referring to me is loaded with potential disapproval. I stood on shaky ground.

I leaned forward and took her hand. "Here it is. I'm going to learn how to skydive and then freefall for a minimum of one mile, and I'm going to do it unassisted."

Jody said nothing, released my hand, stood, and headed to the front door.

"Where are you going? What's the matter?"

"The matter? You mean, 'How does it feel to know that the man I love is determined to kill himself if cancer doesn't?'"

"You know me! I'll plan. I'll prepare. I'll consult experts. I'll practice. I'll reduce the risks to negligible."

"You mean you'll control the risks so they're about the same level of, say, for example, riding your Harley-Davidson without a helmet?"

Ouch.

"Even less, I promise. And I'll also try...to start wearing a helmet. Please don't go."

"Yeah, sure, and that will also be the day the earth stops rotating." Her aura seemed to be growing redder by the second. This woman was so hot, and right then I didn't mean sexually.

"Your sweet mom and I have gone over this I don't know how many times. Neither of us can figure out why you are so persistent about trying to kill yourself with yet another dangerous stunt."

I stood and walked to her with the assertiveness she loves about me. "Hon, it's not about dying. It's about living. I design these experiments to keep me alive longer. I believe they help me fight the genetic mutations that threaten me with tumors. The odds of my cancer returning just jumped a lot higher. The disease has returned after almost forty years of quiescence. So, I want to jump from twelve thousand feet in response. I need the flow. I'll take my time to prepare...not next year, or the year after...but when my mind and body are ready."

She began to cry, something I hadn't seen but one other time when her best friend from high school had died in a tragic car accident the previous summer. "Can't there be a different way—other than risking your life doing something dangerous?"

I encircled her with my arms, hugging her for perhaps thirty seconds without speaking. "Jody, my sweetheart, the lesson I learned forty years ago is that each day is a gift...not just for me but for all of us. I accept this gift with all my being the best way I know how."

Chapter 7

CORONARY

November 2000, University Hospital, Denver, Colorado

I didn't like Bill Smith even though he was my client, a cardiac rehab patient who required more patience than I have ever had. He was a fat, out-of-shape cigarette smoker who whined a lot about what my team was trying to do to help him. He was around my age, but the contrasts between us couldn't have been greater.

He had a beer gut that almost made him look pregnant and skinny legs that walked no farther than from his car into the nearest convenience store where he purchased chili dogs covered with cheese, twenty-ounce bottles of Coke, and packs of Lucky Strike cigarettes. I could theoretically accept extremely unfit patients; I helped them for a living. What I had a lot of trouble tolerating was Bill's acerbic personality: large and in charge, and that rubbed me the wrong way at a deep level. I had never trusted or liked men like him since my six years at St. Mark's, a supreme asshole breeding ground.

Bill founded Strategic Horizons, a software company that helped companies make complex decisions through a process called Monte Carlo simulation. It was all very technical and esoteric, and I tuned out when he tried to explain how the software worked and its applications. Maybe my nonchalant behavior set him off at me—that I did not fawn and gush over his brilliance. A software engineer by training, he was a bright guy and in his own way an extreme risk taker. I could see that his company had been rolling in profits. But I had refused to become one of his minions, paid to stroke his oversized ego. I represented an authority figure messing with his control issues, and when he came into my rehab center he entered my domain.

Bill nearly had a fatal heart attack about one month earlier. He had required emergency cardiac artery bypass grafting. The workup indicated that he had clutched his chest in extreme pain and keeled over at a family cookout that Sunday afternoon; they had rushed him to the University Hospital ER by ambulance. His self-destructive lifestyle had guaranteed severe coronary heart disease with 94 to 96 percent blockages in two coronary arteries. That dude was about one more bacon-wrapped filet mignon away from being a goner.

Bossy and irritating, he expected immediate attention the moment he walked through our doors. Once our nurse checked his basic vitals, he wanted to get on a treadmill and finish as quickly as possible, only he bellyached the whole time he was in rehab. He chewed out two of our staff medical doctors and threatened to sue us at least twice. He didn't follow our recommendations, such as my insistence that he purchase a decent pair of running shoes to replace old brown-leather wingtip dress shoes that he wore to the center. He claimed to be too busy to bother with shopping at a sporting goods store—alien territory for a man whose only understanding of athletic pursuits involved watching Monday Night Football on television while gorging on beers, pretzels, and nachos.

"Bill's here," Candice announced, interrupting me from reading my newest issue of the *Journal of Cardiopulmonary Rehabilitation and Prevention*. "He's pissed."

"What else is new?"

"He's already threatened to quit the program today and report us to administration."

"In a minute. Tell him to cool his jets." I stood and walked over to a mirror above a filing cabinet. Adjusting my tie so it hung straight and tight, I brushed back my hair with my fingers. I tossed on a white lab coat and walked down the hall to one of our exercise rooms where Bill was walking on a treadmill, wired up to an EKG so that we could keep track of his heart functions and detect early signs of cardiac distress.

"How's it going, Bill? You wanted to see me?"

Red faced and sweating profusely, Bill glared at me. "Are you idiots trying to kill me?"

"What do you mean?"

"Look at me! You're supposed to limit my exercise and ease me into this program."

I grabbed his chart from a plastic sleeve nearby and studied his most recent cardiac output readings. "Everything looks okay here. Blood pressure is good. Heart rhythm is almost normal. You're sweating because you're in crummy condition and this is a workout."

"I don't think you people have a clue what you're doing." He wiped sweat off his forehead and rubbed his soaked T-shirt.

"We absolutely know what we're doing. We are pushing you like you've never pushed yourself. Fitness comes at the cost of work. You'll improve. Trust us."

"Trust you! I always feel worse when I leave than when I arrive. My shins hurt all the time. My calf muscles cramp up when I'm asleep—"

"I told you during the intake interview that you're extremely out of shape. Your sedentary lifestyle has weakened your leg muscles as well as your heart. You must exercise all your muscle groups to get in shape, and you'll feel some soreness. That's a good thing—"

"Jocks like you are just macho sadists. You haven't a clue about my pain." He slapped a red emergency button on the treadmill and it stopped.

"I'm not a jock and haven't played team sports since high school. I'm an exercise physiologist. You really need to finish your treadmill workout—"

"I've got customers visiting this afternoon. My presentation is a lot higher priority today—"

"Higher than living?"

"See, that's what I mean. You're just interested in a big paycheck and wearing that self-important white coat, so you can boss patients around."

I became more than irritated with the man, trying hard to manage my anger. I knew I must contain my emotions, but this jerk needed an attitude adjustment. He reminded me of the things I detested about typical competitive corporate men: power hungry, arrogant, insensitive, and self-involved. "I didn't invite you to come here; you invited yourself by smoking, not exercising, and eating all the wrong foods. I understand this is tough for you, but we're not expecting you to do anything you cannot do. This is your life, Bill!"

"My life? I've built a company with three hundred employees, starting with an office in my bedroom at home. We grossed three hundred million last year. This year's going to be even better. That's my life! Not all these wires and this ridiculous torture chamber."

"Reason enough to push through it and make some lifestyle adjustments. Let's take a walk, just you and me."

"What are you going to do?"

"Not a thing other than talk with you. Outside now."

"This is highly irregular. You better not pull anything, or I'll call my attorneys pronto."

"Come on, just follow me. Here, put on your sweatshirt so you don't get a chill." I handed him his gray Harvard sweatshirt (although I heard he had graduated from Colorado State).

The gardens surrounding the hospital had started to die off late in the fall, but it was a brilliant, glorious day, probably in the low seventies. That's what I loved about Denver. When the sun ruled the sky, it was usually pleasant outside even in the middle of winter. We followed a sidewalk encircling some gardens. Many people strolled, while others ate picnic lunches and read books, occupying a few of the available park benches. "I haven't shared this with any of my patients, Bill, but maybe this is a good time."

"Shared what?"

"That I've looked death in the face more times than I can count. But there's one time in particular—"

"Because you're a daredevil? I've heard some gossip about that."

"Death is a scary thing to confront, no doubt about it. It's the great unknown, a mystery waiting at the end of life for all of us."

"That's what I don't need right now, a sermon about the afterlife. Can I smoke out here?" He grabbed a pack of Lucky Strikes from one of his sweatshirt pockets without waiting for my reply. That action almost sent me into an orbit of fury. I hate those damn cancer sticks.

"Not here, you can't. Not anywhere on the hospital grounds."

"Fuck." He stuffed the pack back into a pocket and pulled the hood up over his head. He looked like a fat monk.

I ignored my immediate urge to bash him in the face and continued. "One time I was hunting quail with my uncle and sister. We were in northwestern Kansas around Hays. One of the ranchers out there had been a high school buddy of my uncle. It must have been around six-thirty in the morning with the sun breaking the eastern horizon. My sister, Joanne, and I were just teenagers, eager for the hunt."

"Suddenly a covey of quail flew out of the corn stubble ahead, catching us by surprise. We all aimed at the same time. Both my uncle and sister made their shots, each killing at least one bird. I pulled the trigger and my shotgun exploded in my hands, the end of the barrel peeled back from the force and a few pieces of barrel disappeared, flying who-knows-where."

"Why did it blow up?"

"My uncle instantly recognized his grave error. He had loaded a three-inch cartridge in a gun designed to handle a two-and-three-quarter inch shell. Since he hadn't shot the gun he loaned me for a couple of years, he had forgotten the critical capacity differences between the two shotguns he had loaned us. He had loaded three-inch shells in both of our guns."

"So, what happened to you?"

"I wasn't hurt physically...just shaken. The explosion trashed the gun. But what wounded me was the terrifying awareness that I might have been close to the end of my life. The gun shrapnel could have fatally injured me, or even my sister, who stood nearby. That was a tough lesson for a teenager to learn, a kid who thinks he's immortal.

"I couldn't continue hunting that day even though my uncle had another gun to loan me. He thought I was being a sissy to quit hunting. Joanne razzed me also."

Bill looked over at me as if he saw me for the first time. "Well, I'm with you on this one. I've never been much of a hunter, and I would definitely call it quits if a gun blew up in my hands."

I stopped and nodded at a park bench and we sat. "I was a teenager full of spit and vinegar, a high school athlete and full of myself, but in that moment, I grasped my mortality once again...the kind of awareness that can come to people when they face the harsh possibility of death in such an immediate and dramatic way." I turned and looked at him squarely without trying to be intimidating—I knew that I sometimes threaten men because of my seriousness, bearing and musculature. "Life is precious. Life is short. And life is finite for all of us."

The expression on Bill's face changed from firm to sad. "I know this also. My heart attack rocked my world, making me aware that it's not all about building a company and brandishing an impressive balance sheet. I was scared...I still am scared. I'm not ready to die—"

"That's what this is all about. I'm not pushing you to stop smoking or eat a better diet or work out aerobically because it's some kind of ego-trip for me. I genuinely want to help my patients not only survive their heart attacks but also thrive for years to come. My balance sheet is about having many more healthy and surviving patients than those who don't make it. My commitment to helping patients runs deep. Now you know it comes from a very personal place."

Bill began to weep although I could sense his internal struggle to hold back tears. He probably had not cried in years and certainly not in front of another man he did not trust. "Thriving would be a miracle for me."

I put my hand gently on his shoulder and began to weep with him, dropping all pretense of a professional demeanor, my tears coming from a deep place. "The miracle is our capacity to change and grow. I know a smart, accomplished man like you is capable of extraordinary things. But your future success depends on how you take care of your body today. That's why I'm here, Bill. *I'm here to help.*"

Wiping his eyes with the sleeve of his sweatshirt, he appeared to be experiencing a breakthrough in self-awareness, a moment of deep insight, an *ah-ha experience*. I had seen breakthroughs like this before. I have felt them in myself.

Spring 2003, a private airport near Ft. Collins, Colorado

The sport of skydiving, while not risk free by any means, has a decades-long record of improving safety. In 2002, the year before my planned jump, the United States Parachute Association (USPA) reported thirty-three skydiving fatalities in the United States out of 2.6 million jumps that year. About 85 percent of the skydivers were male, and 15 percent were female. The most likely occupation of the skydivers was military-related (10 percent), followed by, oddly, the computer industry (7 percent).

In recent years, about half-a-million US citizens have given skydiving a try for the first time. More than ten million US citizens can claim they've tried skydiving at least once, so it's an accessible thrill, more popular than you might think if you've never considered it. This experiment would not be as unique as, say, jumping off a bridge, but on the fear scale it was much more momentous to me.

A tandem jump is the easiest and most popular way to experience skydiving for the first time, requiring only about thirty minutes of ground school. Tandem jumping allows novice thrill seekers to experience a freefall from thirteen-thousand feet while attached to an experienced instructor, ostensibly feeling more peace of mind about not screwing up, thus embracing the thrills and sublime freedoms more completely. But I quickly determined that I don't follow the easiest and most popular path in anything I do.

The Accelerated Freefall (AFF) is the next level of challenge. Novice skydivers use a personal parachute system, but two instructors jump simultaneously, stationed on either side of the novice. AFF requires at least a half day of concentrated ground instruction including mastery of body maneuvers and hand signals that instructors use to communicate. The instructors hold onto the newbie's harness until he or she deploys a parachute. This leads to a solo canopy descent with radio instruction to guide the skydiver to a safe landing.

That level presented more of a challenge but still not enough for me. My goal was to achieve a *solo freefall* of at least a mile in length on my first jump, and the USPA normally required new skydivers to complete a minimum of eight or nine skydives to qualify for this degree of jump independence and danger. I wanted to bypass all the intermediate steps and go for the solo freefall the first time I jumped. That elevated the challenge more to my level. If I'm not confronting maximum fear potential, why bother?

As the association cautions: "Skydiving involves inherent risks, but most skydiving accidents result from human error." I knew that minimizing human error in this kind of risk would require a lot more than thirty minutes or four hours of ground school. I planned to take blood chemistries and EKGs in mid-dive. For that kind of biometric information, in return, the USPA gave me special permission to take the freefall plunge on my first dive as long as I took all recommended precautions to minimize risk and a trained instructor jumped with me to provide midflight instructions should something go wrong.

Let me tell you why I was afraid of this experiment almost more than any other I had attempted. It started with my innate survival instinct. Our prehistoric ancestors had the very same instinct—which is why you are alive and reading right now.

A classic study of the fear of heights involved placing an infant on a table. Between this table and another table, the researchers then placed a clear piece of plexiglass. The baby could easily crawl across this plexiglass, but a clear majority of kids refused to the point of crying if pushed or coaxed. That's because clear plexiglass gave these new humans the impression that they could fall and hurt themselves. Baby humans have an innate fear of heights. So do kittens and puppies. So does Luke. Mother Nature built this self-preservation strategy into our DNA.

Jumping off a bridge in a controlled fall is one thing. Jumping into space at 120 mph with thirteen thousand feet between me and the ground is quite another. The act of falling through space, with air blaring in both ears, and without any typical reference points seems unnatural, something humans could not even have contemplated until the invention of human flight at the turn of the twentieth century.

My mental preparation involved cutting out photos of skydivers and pasting them on large aerial photographs of my intended jump zone near Fort Collins, Colorado. I placed these poster boards all over my house, including my bedroom, until Jody became irritated with a frightening aerial view right next to our bed, almost causing her to have vertigo. I watched hours of videos taken from helmet-mounted cameras by skydivers. I would watch these videos while playing peaceful music, thus associating the visual experience with relaxation.

I also took several observation flights to experience skydivers leaping from an airplane and then watched them descend until they became small dots above the fields below. Sometimes I sat in the jump zone and watched final descents and landings as they happened by other skydivers. I absorbed every possible vicarious experience before jumping myself.

My fitness training included miles of running and getting myself into superb aerobic condition while I also practiced yoga to assure flexibility. Sometimes I would run at my maximum speed around ground zero—my eventual landing spot—while imagining myself freefalling through clouds, nary a care in the world. I imagined falling through the clouds and the perfect deployment of my chute. I blocked fearful thinking as much as I could even though the terror of flying lurked in the background, ready to pounce and take control should I become defeatist in my thinking.

One night I had an inevitable nightmare. I was freefalling through air at jet speed, the ground coming closer with each agonizing second. I pulled the ripcord, but no chute deployed. I pulled again. And again. Suddenly I became aware that I would momentarily crash into a junkyard full of rusty automobiles and pieces of steel that would impale me as I crash-landed. I pulled the rip cord again and again without chute deployment. I woke covered with sweat. Thankfully, Jody had slept at her own apartment that night.

My jump day had arrived, and Jody wasn't happy. What else was new?

"I'll still love you if you dump the parachute and leave with me this moment," she insisted. She had come with me to the rural airport near Ft. Collins because I desperately wanted her soothing presence nearby. I then would not have been merely jumping into the void; I would have been jumping into space and returning to her hugs and reassuring kisses.

"Ten people are expecting me to jump. Look around. My support team is standing by. Jamie has handled all the distracting details, so I'm focused. This is not the time to back out. That day came and went forty-eight hours after my thyroidectomy."

"You're such a willful jerk."

"Are you sure you don't want to ride up with me? The pilot and ground school gave their okay."

"Did I mention that I fear flying in little airplanes?"

"I think you did, but this is liberation day: when all good people are to be freed from their flying fears."

"You go ahead and be the liberated one, but I'll be up there with you in spirit. Now...get this thing over with so you can take me out for a gourmet dinner as you promised. Elway's will be fine."

"Deal, hon. I love you."

"Love you. Come back in one piece."

"Check." And with that I walked across the tarmac and climbed into the Cessna, revving and waiting.

After taxiing for a few hundred yards, the plane lifted off the runway, and Chuck, the pilot, gained altitude in graceful circles, banking counterclockwise. Telephone poles became small sticks; giant oak trees became shrubs; the landscape became a checkerboard of crop squares and circles. Purple mountains to the west appeared behind the Front Range. I watched a few cars on a rural county road below me, and they became tiny beetles scurrying along. We quickly gain altitude from three thousand feet to six thousand feet, and soon the Cessna reached terminal altitude of thirteen-thousand feet.

My instructor threw open the door, and without giving the moment any further critical thought, I edged toward the door. He gestured with an *okay* had signal. I visually inspected my harness one more time, making mental note again of the ripcord for the main chute as well as for the emergency shoot. I shifted out into a blast of wind while clasping the wingstrut. My nylon jumpsuit fluttered and snapped, and my ears filled with deafening wind noise. It was a very good thing that I had learned to communicate with my instructor through sign language. Shouting would have gotten us nowhere.

Then I leapt into the air with the arch I had practiced so many times, feeling the slam of air pressure taking control, shaking and jostling, teaching me that a minor hand movement here or a leg change there could completely change the direction and momentum of my flight. I continued arching my back so that my center of gravity remained stable as the airstream rushed between my outstretched fingers. An imbalance here, a compensating gesture there. I felt immediately in control of the freefall, a master of diving through sky. My freefalling instructor showed me a thumbs-up to assure me that the dive was proceeding as planned.

My perceptions of velocity became magnified by shrill whistles filling my helmet. I saw the earth rushing toward me as small houses grew and became resolved in detail. Black Hollow Reservoir, which had looked like a pond when I jumped, suddenly appeared more like a lake. A gray-green roof on a country market became a bright green roof as I felt closer. That single mile of freefall flashed by in moments, and my instructor signaled that I must pull the pilot shoot. I pulled the ripcord and—nothing happened.

The parachute was not deploying. I tried again, and again. Another thousand feet rushed past me. Then another. Then another. I felt relaxed, almost Zen-like in my response to this dangerous turn of events. The free-floating feeling had become almost hypnotic; I felt *the flow*. I could have surrendered to this freedom like no earth-bound creature can entirely appreciate. No anxieties. No regrets. An ingenious twenty-four-hour monitoring package I had helped invent wrapped my waist and measured my blood chemistry and heart functions as I fell toward the drop zone.

My instructor became much less sanguine about my surrendering to the moment. I could not be certain what he had signaled me to do because his gestures weren't the same as those we had practiced. Another thousand feet zoomed past me, and I judged that the ground was less than three-thousand feet below. I could see my team and even tiny Jody in her red T-shirt standing near the drop zone. The instructor motioned his thumb upward. He frenetically exaggerated his body movements for me to look up, to lift my head and look up and behind me as if trying to find the Cessna that had taken us above the clouds. I looked up. Nothing. He threw back his head and looked up again. Dutifully I copied him with more exaggeration in my movement, and the pilot parachute snapped into existence. Then an insight came to me about my predicament, an understanding stemming from my hours of study and preparation. My wide shoulders had created a vacuum, allowing my uninflated chute to remain on my back. Once I had looked up with enough force, the airstream rushed over my shoulders and enabled the chute to unfurl as it should.

The final part of my journey involved graceful circling, sailing over all that seemed familiar and the one who really cared waiting for me on terra firma. I soared silently on subtle air currents as the landing zone gradually filled my field of vision, and my feet performed a perfect two-point touchdown, just as I had imagined when Harley and I had run together in City Park almost ten years earlier.

Jody ran over to me, a combination of fear and anger in her expression. "What the hell kept you from releasing your parachute?"

"My shoulders created a microvacuum. Everything turned out fine."

"I can't take this anymore. If you want me around, then you've got to stop taking these stupid risks." Members of my team sensed that things had become tense between Jody and me and stayed back. She probably had warned them to keep their distance.

"Why would you impose restrictions on me now?"

"We've been through this before. I want you around next year, and in five years, and even in thirty years. I want a partner for the long run, not a sprint."

"Hon, you don't want to live with a caged animal. They become mean and unpredictable."

"Why do you make it so hard?"

I grabbed her shoulders. "You are part of this journey!"

"Listen to me. I can't take this anymore. I don't want to stand around helpless and watch you die. I don't want to live with someone obsessed with planning feats all the time." She removed my hands from her shoulders with a look of defiance that I loved so much about her. She could be a *hard-headed woman*, as the song intoned.

"Life is short. Life is finite. Nobody has been promised tomorrow. In chaotic situations, I'm in control. In uncertainty, I'm free."

"We'll celebrate your parachute opening over dinner. But we're not finished with this discussion." She gave me a quick hug and a peck on my cheek, turned and walked toward my car.

I had soared beyond the predictable, mundane routines of life once again, experiencing another terrifying joy that this temporal existence offers those willing to accept the gift of risk-taking. In those precious moments of freefalling freedom, I had gained greater control of my destiny. Check off another item on my fear list. Cancer had nothing and everything to do with a most memorable day.

Chapter 8

RIVER

Fall 2003, Washington Park, Denver, Colorado

Jody ran next to me with grace and athleticism. Her long, lean legs kept pace with my wider stride, and she seemed unfazed by my tendencies to compete by increasing my cadence unconsciously. I reminded myself to ease back and not turn this casual run around Washington Park into an Olympic competition. She would compete if challenged. Maintaining a slower jogging pace allowed us to talk about things we sometimes avoided or ignored when we were not exercising. I found our runs together to be the best time for us to share our hearts without pretense or self-censorship.

The park was almost empty at 6:17 a.m., and that was part of the reason we picked this time. An early alarm got us up and out during the coolest time of the day, and we didn't need to negotiate our way around slower joggers, parents walking children in strollers, runners with dogs on leashes, and many others rambling around the park's perimeter path. We could run side-by-side without needing to be wary of accidental collisions.

It was still dark with the sun rising later in fall. We could just make out the running path because the first light of dawn finally touched the eastern sky. The air felt biting with temperatures hovering in the low fifties. But the humidity felt low, and the crisp air energized us. I became tempted to kick into high gear but caught myself again to avoid an inevitable running race.

"I love the stillness of this time of day," she said.

"So do I. Do you ever pray when you experience these pastoral moments?"

"Not often. I just don't think about it." She glanced at me with a question. "Do you?"

We then ran next to a small pond that had been adopted by a flock of ruddy ducks. Their quiet quacks added to my bucolic feelings, a sense that nature has a purpose far greater than we can imagine or understand. We are connected to the larger web of life, and sometimes it is easy for us to forget that humans are part of nature, not above it.

Our jogging rhythm had become lockstep, each of us leading with the same leg—left, right...left, right...left, right—a cadence that made me feel even more linked to this remarkable person, as if we had become a single athletic organism.

"Luke, I asked if you ever pray while we're running."

"Almost all the time when we're not speaking."

"That surprises me."

"Why, Jody?"

"Well, you're not the church-going type, that's for sure."

"True, organized religion has never been helpful for me." My mind fabricated a musty chapel at St. Mark's, a dreaded place that had felt alien, and, in retrospect, hypocritical. I had hated Sunday services and the long-winded, moralistic sermons delivered by a chaplain with his monotonous oratory. I had hated being anywhere near that dog killer, Sarge Deville.

"Can we stop and walk awhile? I'm sure we've run at least five kilometers by now."

"Yes, let's take the path around the pond. It will reflect the beautiful dawn light."

She grabbed my hand and held it tightly. "Whom do you pray to?"

It struck me then that we had never had a deeper spiritual discussion in our years as a couple. How odd this topic had not come up with any depth. There had been passing mentions of God and a few perfunctory prayers during family meals with my daughters, but that was all so far. "I pray to the divine force that has created all this: pond, ducks, Washington Park, you, and me."

"A divine being?"

"Yes, an infinite and benevolent force of which our spirits are a part." Another jogger passed us and waved without speaking. This was truly the best time of day for solitude. "I sense this eternal presence throughout the day. This gives me great strength and comfort."

"I'm a little surprised that you're so spiritual. You're certainly not overt about it." She removed a rubber band from her hair, which had been pulled into a ponytail, shook her head, and allowed her soft dishwater-blonde hair to fall to her shoulders. As always, her sensuality enlivened me. "Are you checking me out again?"

"Yes. That's one way I appreciate our creator: your seductive body and vibe."

She giggled and squeezed my hand again. "Then what happens to us after we die?"

"I'm no closer to knowing the answer to that question than have been many of the greatest mystics and philosophers. I can only speculate about something over which living humans will never get a complete answer. I sense this journey to eternity will be benevolent and give us a peace that we mortals seek and never find. Our lives are defined by struggle. Death ends struggle, a final blessing."

"Okay, I finally get it. You fill your life with struggles to make the end of struggles even more rewarding. Like that little river swim you're planning?"

I loved how she challenged me. A lesser man would have been offended or become defensive because Jody never allowed actions and choices to go unnoticed or unquestioned. "I looked squarely at death near the beginning of my life when I was just eight. I knew that my time here would be limited no matter how many more years I have. Even those humans with the longest lives still pass through this mortal plane in a blink when considering the cosmological context: this four-billion-year-old planet and the thirteen-billion-year-old cosmos. I realized so young that I must use my time with purpose and a competitive spirit to win all of the confrontations that might test me." Realizing that I had been cross-examined by a master prosecutor, I turned the question back upon her. "What about you? Don't you ever seek the peace and reconciliation that can come with prayer?"

She continued walking without answering, as if I had asked something off-limits.

"You can share with me, hon. Please."

"You know I was raised as a Catholic, and my early childhood years involved much devotion to the church. I attended mass and confession all the time. I especially liked learning about the Christian faith through bible study—"

Her voice trailed off as if she had traveled someplace else. We started walking at a slower pace although she released my hand. I had learned by then not to push too far into the mysterious corners of her life. She was the kind of person who sometimes set invisible psychological boundaries not to be crossed. But this was fundamental and important. "You haven't attended a mass since I've known you. Did something happen?"

"Yes, damn it, something happened." She paused to gather her thoughts or summon courage. "When I was eleven I went to the church one Saturday to help decorate for the holidays. Ten or twelve kids my age were there also. We had a lot of fun with a visiting young priest who made the decorating amusing. He sang silly songs and teased us.

"At the end of the day, other parents had picked up their children. My dad was late. The priest lulled me into a conversation and told me how much he loved my enthusiasm and peppy attitude. He asked for a hug that didn't stop there. He touched me inappropriately and fondled me. He put his large hand down my underpants and assaulted me with perverted sexual petting. Then he made me promise not to tell anyone or I would risk excommunication."

Intense feelings of anger overwhelmed me. "Did you share this with your father or some other adult?"

"No, this was the seventies and I had nowhere to go with the truth about such an up-and-coming priest. I don't think I would have been able to articulate what had happened to me. I was suspicious that I might be blamed, as if I had seduced him in some sick, prepubescent way. The experience became my private shame and eventually led to my alienation and withdrawal from the church."

We stopped, and I peered into her eyes, which sparkled with early morning light. "God, I'm so sorry, Jody. I'd like to find that priest and make his day a living hell."

"He's already in hell—killed in a car accident about ten years ago. That divine force of yours must have interceded."

I encircled her with my arms, and she did not resist. I knew our relationship had reached a new level because of her sharing something so full of pain and shame, something so deeply personal. I also knew the details of her molestation would probably never be forthcoming. I understood better why she was so assertive. "My divine force does not intervene in our lives. But it's a presence that we can access when we need forgiveness and consolation. Will you just pray with me now? Not to the Catholic god. Or the Muslim or Jewish god. But to the God in your heart. The divine force that's part of you."

We hugged in silence, other runners and walkers passing us. I had loved this woman for many reasons during our courtship and the gradual maturation of our relationship. But I loved her more in that moment than I have words to describe. That may have been our spiritual wedding, the moment we connected and intertwined for eternity. I prayed that our divine creator would give her acceptance, peace, and transcendence.

No child should face a brutal beginning in life, whether confronting sexual exploitation by a priest or ravages of childhood cancer. Jody and I had become as one.

Fall 2004, Missouri River between Kansas City and St. Louis

In the nineteenth century, the problem was that God is dead; in the twentieth century, the problem is that man is dead. In the nineteenth century inhumanity meant cruelty; in the twentieth century, it means schizoid self-alienation. The danger of the past was that men became slaves. The danger of the future is that men may become robots. True enough, robots do not rebel. But, given man's nature, robots cannot live and remain sane, they become unfinished human beings that will destroy their world and themselves because they cannot stand any longer the boredom of a meaningless life.

— Erich Fromm

I had memorized this passage from Erich Fromm's *The Sane Society*, which he published in 1955. I often ended my speeches by reciting this quotation from the twentieth century sociologist as a way of summing up my deepest convictions. Fromm celebrated the virtue of humans acting independently and employing reason to establish moral values rather than adhering to received authority from others, a characteristic trap of modern life in complex societies.

Fromm can be ponderous to read and understand. But I had come to appreciate his message in my own rudimentary ways. Embracing freedom of will is healthy; using escape mechanisms is the root of psychological illnesses.

Humans can escape personal freedom in at least three ways. First, they change their ideal self to conform to society's preferred personalities. We know society has little tolerance for its artistic individualists who shun typical and expected behaviors and lifestyles. Second, they displace the burden of choice to society. This escape, I believe, is the root of all the blame games: when things don't work out in life, blame a parent, blame the government, blame corporations, or blame someone else to avoid taking personal responsibility for making a choice and for its outcome. And, third, they submit their freedom to others: let someone in higher authority tell us how to feel or react. Karl Mannheim, another twentieth century sociologist and peer of Fromm's, observed how society can force us to assume "collective mentalities" or dominant ways of thinking—intrinsic values so widely shared that they become almost beyond reproach.

So many of my fellow humans have chosen negative risks and have adopted poor health habits, such as my patient Bill Smith who danced with the devil every time he lit up another cigarette or gobbled down a convenience store chili dog swimming in artery-clogging cheddar cheese. Millions like Bill have followed his path to self-destruction. Although by the late nineties, cigarette smoking had been culturally demoted from aspirational behavior to a pathetic addiction in the eyes of the majority, overeating and overdrinking remained revered through modern advertising and popular culture. Erich Fromm would have had us understand that attractiveness and acceptance of dysfunctional behaviors does not make vices into virtues. He called this "pathological normalcy."

Fromm concluded that "destruction of the world is the last, almost desperate attempt to save myself from being crushed by it." And so our species may be destroying our mother, evident for several decades with the escalating severity of cataclysmic weather, global warming, and population overgrowth.

These were indeed heady thoughts for someone swimming nonstop from Kansas City to St. Louis in the Missouri River, a

375-mile water marathon, unprecedented as far as anyone could recall. This was my freedom in action: a "nut job" who could dress and pose as a model for the cover of *Gentlemen's Quarterly* magazine but instead had chosen to don a wetsuit and spend his days floating and swimming in muddy waters, exposed to physical dangers, extreme stress, and hypothermia. This was indeed a perfect time of night to fill the hours with contemplation of the choices I had made and have been making, a turn away from that which is expected of me, Dr. Luke, and that which I have chosen to accomplish so I can help others follow my example and make the most of their brief time to exist.

Place me in the context of Bill Smith, then: his chosen lifestyle involved negative risks, assuring illnesses and premature death. No matter how large and successful his software company could become, Bill had chosen the lifestyle of a loser. My life involved taking positive risks, calculated and managed, so that I could achieve success and in the long run become healthier—physically, emotionally, and spiritually—than had I never tried to test myself. Have I been extreme in demonstrating this? To many, yes. *Could my experiments become metaphors for life's winners?* I believed so.

That explained why I had become frigid, why my support boat remained at least four hundred yards behind me as instructed, and why I was willingly exposing myself to more media scrutiny with the possibilities of my failures being broadcast to an amused, unsympathetic, nacho-gorging media audience. It was also why I warily looked out for channel catfish weighing over a hundred pounds, surprise whirlpools, poisonous snakes, strings of fishhooks thrown across the river to catch channel cat, unseen junk lurking below the surface to impale me, rambling barges, and rumored quicksand.

We had been delayed in getting started on this adventure, which I had hoped would get underway in early October. Now that the first week of November had arrived, the water temperature of fifty-five degrees could quickly facilitate hypothermia, a dramatic lowering of body temperature. Shivering is the best understood symptom, but this is only the tip of the iceberg, if you'll excuse my pun. Hypothermia also contributes to shallow breathing, a weak pulse, abnormal heart rhythms, lack of coordination, confusion, poor decision making, drowsiness, very low energy, lack of concern about a deteriorating condition, loss of consciousness, and, of course, death.

I wore an insulated wetsuit and had applied a copious mixture of Vaseline and lanolin to my skin, but shivering had been haunting me all night, and my support team, led by Jody and Jamie, had checked in with me about every thirty minutes by asking me questions and assessing the lucidity of my answers. As if a phantasmagoria emerging from darkness, the rubber pontoon boat glided up beside me again.

"How are you doing, hon?" she asked with bright enthusiasm in her voice.

"I'm thinking clearly about many things, including why we must take risks."

"Heady thoughts!"

"Exactly my thinking as well. Are you and the team doing okay?"

"It's damn cold out here, a few degrees lower than water temperature."

I began a gentle breaststroke to keep my circulation active. That takes more effort than just floating in the main channel of the river, but I understood that I must continue willing my large muscles to move. "It's supposed to warm up tomorrow. Right?"

"That's correct, Luke. The forecast calls for a high in the low sixties and sunny all day."

"Thank God. I'm not sure I can stand much more of this cold."

"Time to eat." Jody gently set a Styrofoam tray on the water and nudged it my direction.

"Oh, joy. I'm going to have to force some of this down. I'm simply not hungry."

"That's Mr. Hypothermia knocking. You must eat everything on the tray. No excuses."

Reluctantly, I pushed the tray in front of me, hand feeding myself from a bounty of whole wheat bread slathered with almond butter; dried fruits such as figs, raisins, and dates; farmer's cheese for more low-cholesterol fat; and some glorious dark chocolate. I had been burning about eight thousand calories every day, so frequent and plentiful feedings were essential for my success.

Jody had stowed a boom box on the pontoon boat, and she played a wonderful mixture of classic rock. The music helped me to stop noticing my immediate discomfort and allowed me to become transported to other places, whether to a country farm with Crosby Stills and Nash or a warm, sandy California beach with The Beach Boys. The meal and musical interlude knocked off another five miles of my journey, which would require at least five days and nights. I felt warmer, as much because of the food as because of the attention and love coming from my crew.

As the days passed, I challenged monotony with games. We had packed several hundred tennis balls to throw in the water ahead of us, so we could easily find the main water channel. Members of my support team threw tennis balls ahead of me, which I swam for and tried to grab, and, when successful with recovery, I threw the balls back, trying to hit one of them. This game of tennis dodge ball filled hours with laughter and play and accelerated our progress, transforming arduous physical challenges into games. Play makes work disappear, and amusement can be found in any work.

Near the junction of the Gaconade River and the Missouri, about ninety miles from St. Louis, we pulled over near a riverside park to meet one of our crew members who had driven a van stocked with provisions. This was the first time I had been out of water in over four days, and my body experienced an enlivening weight of gravity. The full mass of my body felt wonderful after so many days of floating and swimming in dirty liquid.

While my team handled operational issues, I approached an older gentleman who was sitting idly on a park bench watching our crew with enormous curiosity. He ogled my wetsuit as if I was a creature from the black lagoon. "A beautiful day, mister."

Dribbling tobacco juice from the corners of his mouth, his walnut face lined with deep crevices from a lifetime of working outdoors, he shifted uncomfortably. "Where ya headin'?"

"St. Louis."

"Where ya been?"

"Kansas City."

"Young feller, you mean you been swimming all the way from KC?"

"Yes sir, I have."

"Ya don't get in that boat with the rest of 'em?"

"No sir. This is an experiment to test my strength and stamina."

"Well, I never—"

"Our goal is not far from here, about ninety more miles."

"Why would ya do such a thing?"

"Well, it's a little hard to explain. But I'm trying to demonstrate that we can achieve our dreams by setting risky goals, planning, and then persevering through all the obstacles."

"Are you some kind of daredevil?"

"Not really. I plan and prepare for months, sometimes years. I consult with experts. I minimize the risks."

"What do they call ya?"

"Luke."

"I'm Bond, Walter Bond."

The dissimilarities between Walter and James were quite ironic and ridiculous, and I giggled.

"What's so darn funny?"

"Nothing important. I just noticed that you have the same last name as my childhood hero, James Bond, you know, the British secret agent."

"I've heard that one before." Walter leaned over and spat out a mouthful of brown saliva. "And it's not too far from the truth either. I was a spy in World War II."

A bit dumbfounded and conscious of my stereotypical assumptions about this old man, I sat next to him, so he could tell me more of his story. I learned that he had acted as a spy in German-occupied France. His French language skills were impeccable, belying his folksy ways of speaking English. His descriptions cascaded in and out of French dialect, which I did not understand but in context.

He told me that after months of posing as a French bartender in a pub near Strasberg in eastern France close to the German border, he had been able to steal some important battle plans from a valise left unattended by a drunken German officer. Traveling across country at night while avoiding several direct and lethal confrontations with the enemy, he had been able to return to his unit, which had by then established its operations at Rouen during the early weeks after the Allied invasion of Normandy. James Bond he was not, but an American hero—yes, most definitely. For that act of enormous strategic importance and the courage to travel solo behind enemy lines for over five hundred miles, he had been awarded the Bronze Star Medal, the fourth-highest combat award of the US Armed Forces.

And I thought: *Floating and swimming downstream during peacetime for 375 miles is an impressive achievement?*

Jody waved me back to the shore. "Thank you for sharing your story with me, Walter. My team needs me to get back in the water. It's time to swim again so we can stay on schedule. Thank you for your service and sacrifices."

He shook my hand and nodded his appreciation. "Don't you get too cold in that water, but it looks like you know what yer doin'."

"Thanks. I'll be careful. Great to meet you, sir."

"Dieu vitesse et un bon voyage, mon ami." He waved and leaned over and spat again.

Throughout the cloudless and starry night that followed this remarkable encounter with someone all my preparation had not anticipated, I studied the constellations above and reflected upon my first reaction to Walter. I must be truthful. I had concluded that he must have been an ignorant, unkempt, and unremarkable person—just another irrelevant old man wiling away his remaining days on a park bench overlooking a muddy, undulating river. Considering the extraordinary care that my grandmother had given me as a child when I struggled with so many health challenges—my mother busy entertaining in Las Vegas—it seemed that I should not have been so quick to "judge a book by its cover." My grandmother had been old and wrinkled, same as Walter, and yet her wisdom informed my destiny in so many ways. She had taught me about health and commitment and self-sufficiency. Walter was a gift, as are all the humans who reach his age after years of working, contributing, and sacrificing to make a difference for others. I prayed and promised my divine being that I would be more vigilant about monitoring my prejudices when they appear and then systematically eliminating them from my psyche. This represented the same kind of mental preparation and discipline that had enabled me to undertake an atavistic journey through geologic time, floating unconstrained with the currents of a great river to a deeper sense of myself.

When we spotted the St. Louis skyline in the late morning of day six, I also finally saw the Gateway Arch, a symbol of the nation's pioneering, risk-taking spirit—an exceptional nation that Walter Bond and his generation had defended decades earlier.

Chapter 9

BREATHE

March 2006, Highline Canal, Denver, Colorado

Harley and I loved to run along the Highline Canal, a landmark irrigation system completed in 1883 to deliver mountain snowmelt and rain runoff throughout the Denver metro area. An asphalt and gravel trail follows all sixty-six miles of the canal, winding through many parks and secluded neighborhoods. My loyal fur-person learned to tolerate a leash, as required by city ordinance, although he would have preferred the pure freedom of no constraints. Wouldn't we all?

I began most of our runs near Cherry Creek Country Club and followed the trail all the way to Fairmont Cemetery where we would rest and recover, often with a slow stroll among the burial monuments while consuming energy snacks (dog cookies for Harley) before returning to my car. That worked out to about seven miles total running distance. You'd think Harley would have tuckered out, but he was so full of energy and enthusiasm that he never seemed haggard during our runs. He had been known to take a brief power nap at Fairmont while I wandered among the gravesites, but he bounced back for return runs to my car. All it took was an insistent, guttural statement of his name, and—bam! — he would be up and running.

The expansive 275-acre cemetery is one of Denver's oldest fully operational burial sites, and many famous Colorado pioneers are at rest there. One burial stone fascinated me. The stone marks the grave of Madeline Alex Bleakley and carries a haunting or humorous message, depending on your point of view:

Finally having a good day.

This ambiguous epithet could be the concluding message of someone with a macabre sense of humor, or that of a very religious person (now with her savior), or it could be the final message of a sad woman who had not experienced much joy in life. I chose the first interpretation: that her death came with irony, a tongue-in-cheek manner of laughing her way to her grave. I often stopped and lingered near her gravesite and contemplated whether I was feeling then that life could be so difficult and challenging that I would welcome my passage into eternity with a wry smile and a wink of relief—effectively, a kiss off—a fair question for mortals to periodically contemplate. I knew for certain that my life had been filled with thrills, chills, and spills, rarely boring or dreary. Madeline and I had little in common when it came to summing up life and contemplating eternity.

I have also thought about my burial monument epithet without sharing these ruminations with anyone until this written reflection. I think my most consistent answer to that inevitable, final decision could be succinct and direct:

A warrior who fought for life.

And that pretty much sums me up: I have brought the heart and courage of a warrior to all my challenges throughout life, whether recovering from disease and injury, pursuing a challenging academic career, planning and executing endurance experiments, or being a professional exercise physiologist and sports psychologist.

At every stage I have fought all the forces that could have deterred or detoured less committed people, those who fear daring and resist new challenges. I am proud of this but not arrogant. I am humbled by my tenacious spirit because I see this aspect of my personality as fragile and temporal. I doubt that I will ever shy away from self-imposed challenges, but I will lose a final battle. As will you. As will all of us. So, as the years have rolled by and I have continued to confront diminishing physicality, I have become more resolute and less willing to accept that the instant of resignation is now, this moment. To Madeline I always silently whispered, "This day is a good day, Maddy. I'm happy to be alive. Every living day is a good day, no matter the challenges or emotions that may come my way."

Nose attached to the vegetation next to the Highline Canal trail, Harley seemed more exuberant this day than most. Our run had been easy and swift with few other canine distractions. Like most dogs, Harley must approach and smell other dogs that he encounters, and I inevitably become engaged in dog discussions with human owners. This slows our pace and limits the flow of running that I prefer to achieve. Since it was just after sunup on a Sunday in March, the vigorous chill and early time of day made our running trail peaceful and empty.

I had been struggling with a chest cold for several days, which surprised me. I never get colds or the flu because of an extraordinary immune system. Perhaps childhood battles with cancer and my grandmother's careful ministrations with folk medicines, herbal healing, and vitamin therapies had infused my system with an overabundance of macrophages and phagocytes. I am around sick people all the time and never get sick myself. I've survived several of Jody's vicious colds without catching a virus from her. But on this day my throat had felt raspy and I kept coughing an annoying, dry cough.

With a lot of doggedness, while disregarding my persistent sputtering, I nudged Harley along and into the cemetery where we ran past one of the tallest monuments in the burial community paying tribute to Dr. John Evans. We reached my anticipated resting spot, the tomb of an extraordinary woman. Because of her interesting name and the prominence of her final resting place on the cemetery grounds, I had searched her name on the Internet to learn something about her.

Dr. Hannah Marie Wormington had been one of the first women in the United States to build a career in archeology and had become an internationally acclaimed expert on the paleo-Indian period. She had written several books and dozens of articles for scientific publications. Two of her best-known books were *Ancient Man in North America* (1939) and *Prehistoric Indians of the Southwest* (1947). She had been affiliated with the Denver Museum of Natural History for nearly six decades. She died in 1994 due to a fire in her home. Ironically, the cause of her death at age seventy-nine had been smoke inhalation: she had apparently started a fire by smoking a cigarette and then fallen asleep before extinguishing her final cancer stick.

Smoking kills.

In the spirit-company of this notable scholar and former cigarette smoker, I began to cough uncontrollably, a full-chest whoop from deep within my lungs. I could not recall when I had coughed so much. Harley looked alarmed at the noise coming from his master, and he began to whine. I sputtered to him that I was okay, but clearly, I was not okay. From deep within my lungs I coughed phlegm and dark clots of blood. I knew without any hesitation that something could be very wrong with me.

I could not run any more that day, and so we walked slowly back to my car, a return journey seemed to take hours. My upper left chest felt tight, and my coughing and wheezing continued. Harley appeared most concerned, lagging behind me without any attempts to dart off and greet other dogs that we came across along the way back. The drive home became equally discomforting, and I walked into our home to find Jody drinking coffee by a gas fireplace in the living room.

She glanced at me and her eyes registered concern. "What happened to you?"

"Something is wrong with my left lung." I hesitated a moment to search her inquisitive face. "I coughed up some blood."

She stood and walked across the room and studied my face, checking my forehead for a fever. "We need to get you to your doctor—today."

"It's Sunday."

"I could care less," she insisted. "Coughing up blood is a major warning sign. You know that. He gave you his cell phone number. Call him."

"I hate to bother him on a Sunday."

She grabbed my face with both hands and stared into my eyes with her no-compromises clinical gaze. "Call him. You need medical attention today, not tomorrow."

I have learned many times over that it is of little use to argue with Jody about health issues. She was accustomed to being authoritative with patients and their families. She did not allow tentative and noncommittal reactions to her instructions. She could make any attending physician nervous. So, I clutched my cell phone and punched in the single speed dial digit for my oncologist.

Have I got your undivided attention yet, Luke?

You already know me well after all these years, but please allow me to reintroduce myself. In my most recent reincarnation, I am known as *large cell undifferentiated carcinoma*—or just *lung cancer* for sake of brevity. I am undisputedly a serious malady.

You see, my fellow tribe members of the Large Cell Undifferentiated Lung Cancer Clan (LCULCC) are responsible for 28 percent of all cancer deaths each year, and LCULCC carcinomas like me account for 10 to 15 percent of *all lung cancer cases*. We are badass carcinomas who love to grow rapidly, spreading like crabgrass in Arkansas to affect other areas of your body. Even with treatment your prognosis is dismal: the five-year survival rate in cases where we have metastasized is only a measly 3 percent.

Too bad, so sad.

You might think I'm an ugly fellow if you choose to look at me, but I'm quite handsome in a grotesque kind of way. I'm a pink-gray mass about the size of an egg with extensive bleeding and substantial cell death in my interior. Lots of blood vessels have been collecting and collaborating to feed my voracious appetite for sugar.

You've been aware of my rude interruptions of your daily life, especially a fitness freak like you. It's axiomatic that even smart guys choose to ignore my warning signs.

How's that working for you, Dr. Luke?

You know I've been lurking for weeks with your escalating coughing and shortness of breath, not to mention dark brown blood splotches floating in the phlegm you've been choking up. You've felt tired with less effort, falling asleep earlier at night when you usually prefer to read and write. You've dropped a few pounds, haven't you? A lean dude with 12 percent body fat notices a few pounds shedding away. You know your weight loss is at the expense of that lean muscle you've worked so hard to build, and how you hate to lose muscle!

That brilliant oncologist of yours (also my sworn enemy) is going to recommend something radical and daring. No wimpy surgery for you. We're not talking about wedge resection, where the guy with the scalpel cuts me out and removes some surrounding lung tissue for extra precaution. No, you're going to get a kick-ass knife job: a lobectomy. That's where a lobe or section of your lung is removed. I think in your case two lobes will suffice. And don't you dare feel sorry for yourself about the surgical treatment plan; you could be looking at a pneumonectomy, where an entire lung is ripped from its host. (Two lobes or an entire lung: pretty much the same difference.)

But, alas, all the pain and weakness you'll face during rehab are to no avail. Like you, Lukey Boy—oops, old habit, guess you're not a boy anymore—like you, I have a wandering spirit. I like to move around energetically. I prefer to search for remote locations to set up shop, such as a brain, liver, or lymph system, but I haven't quite made up my mind yet where I should take my next foreign holiday. I have a bucket list, and just about every organ in your body offers intriguing possibilities for my future travel plans.

Why you, why now? I'll try not to be pedantic. Smoking is the greatest risk factor to attract the brethren of LCULCC tribe. Such a cruel irony it is that you have never smoked a single cigarette in your life. But we also owe our divine creation to radiation, air pollution, second-hand smoke, and sundry environmental toxins pervading human habitation: asbestos, tar, soot, arsenic, and other industrial crap too numerous to point out.

But did I mention radiation? Bingo!

April 2006, University Hospital, Denver, Colorado

Dr. Sen, my gentle, dark-skinned Indian doctor, a professional's professional, put me through a carousel of medical tests including a computerized axial tomography (CAT) scan; a bronchoscopy, a procedure that allowed the pulmonary specialist to study the inside of my left lung with a small camera attached to a tube, which they had inserted through my nose; and a panel of blood tests requiring what seemed like two pints of blood. As with all invasive medical testing, I felt exhausted and slightly light-headed due to the lingering effects of a mild anesthesia they had used during the bronchoscopy.

Dr. Sen walked into the examination room where I had been waiting with Jody for several hours. His expression was grave, and I knew he wasn't bringing us good news.

Jody stood and walked over to him, her bearing direct and no-nonsense. "What have we learned, doctor?"

Dr. Sen answered her question with equal medical directness. "When Dr. Cohen conducted Luke's bronchoscopy, he found a mass about the size and shape of an egg. The mass is blocking his left bronchi."

He turned away from Jody's intense stare and looked at me. "The pathology report from the biopsy reveals that the mass is cancerous. I'm sorry to share this news, Luke."

When presented with bad medical news, I become clinical and detached, part of my own medical training in exercise physiology and cardiac rehabilitation. "Then what are you recommending?"

"Our team's opinion is that we must remove the tumor as soon as we can schedule surgery—"

"You'll remove just the tumor?" Jody demanded, her hands on her hips, revealing her commanding demeanor, which made her look taller than she already is, especially when standing next to this diminutive oncologist.

Dr. Sen hauntingly glanced from Jody to me and back at her. "We also recommend removal of about three-fourths of Luke's left lung. Cancer cells are dividing rapidly. This is a virulent form of lung cancer called large-cell undifferentiated carcinoma. Partial lung removal is one way we can retard further metastases."

Years of physical training have also toughened me to withstand the worst of news. "How soon?"

"Well, Luke, we can get this scheduled for next week. You'll be in the hospital for about ten days."

"I need a month before surgery."

Jody looked at Sen and insisted, "Schedule it next week."

I looked at Jody and persisted, "I've got work to do to get my body ready, hon."

"Luke! This cancer is growing and spreading inside you now."

"I love you, but this is my body and my life. I'm drawing the line here. One month."

Dr. Sen looked at both of us and shrugged, "My assistant will schedule Luke's surgery for as close to one month from today as possible. Dr. Jim Peterson will be my recommendation for your surgeon. Are you okay with this?"

Jody appeared relieved. "Jim's got a great reputation." She looked at me, shifting quickly from a no-nonsense authority to my sweet love. "Okay. We'll do it your way, but I'm involved in every step of this journey. Okay?"

I nodded and reached for her hand. Dr. Sen smiled and rushed out of the room without further comment, characteristic of his low-key, accepting nature.

I spent a month engaged in a rigorous fitness regimen to prepare myself for lung surgery and rapid postoperative recovery. I ran five days each week with Harley, burning up the trail along the Highline Canal. Coughing up bloody phlegm just became part of the routine. I ignored tightness in my chest and shortness of breath. When pain increased, I ran faster. Harley loved it.

Jody made sure I ate a textbook vegetarian diet with meals prepared from organic foods and large portions of vegetables and fruits. Soy-based products and legumes provided over one hundred grams of daily protein intake to facilitate healthy tissue maintenance and growth. I consumed a gallon each of carrot and spinach juice every day. I lifted weights, especially emphasizing upper body routines with knowledge that those would be my final days lifting. The invasiveness of that surgery required the surgeon to break through my ribs, and this made it more than likely that I would never again enjoy another bench press of 250 or more pounds. (I am, you know, an exercise physiologist.) I meditated as typical of my prior encounters with cancer, visualizing my body's white blood cells engulfing and then destroying tumor cells.

I chose to cast my fate both to traditional Western medicine but in combination with other fringe treatments that were showing promise. One of those therapies involved administration of tens of thousands of milligrams of ascorbic acid or Vitamin C directly into my blood stream. My friend, the chiropractor, hooked me up twice weekly with an intravenous administration of high doses of the vitamin. My decision, admittedly borne of intense emotion about self-control, had also been scientifically validated.

When large amounts of vitamin C are presented to cancer cells intravenously, the cells absorb the vitamin. The antioxidant qualities of vitamin C start behaving as a pro-oxidant as the vitamin interacts with intracellular trace metals such as copper and iron. High doses of vitamin C continue to build up until eventually causing cancer cells to decompose from the inside out, a process called apoptosis. The vitamin stimulates collagen formation to help the body wall off the tumor and assist with postoperative tissue repair. The vitamin inhibits hyaluronidase, an enzyme that tumors employ to metastasize and invade other organs. This makes high-dose IV-C a nontoxic and chemotherapeutic agent that can be given safely in conjunction with conventional cancer treatments.

Intravenous vitamin C does more than just kill cancer cells. It can also boost immunity and facilitate the speed of postoperative recovery. Cancer patients become exhausted and lethargic, bruise easily, and have reduced hunger, leading to the characteristic weight loss that you may have associated with the dreaded disease. Cancer patients often don't sleep well and some of us have a low pain threshold.

Research studies are showing that when cancer patients receive intravenous C before major surgeries, they report reduced levels of pain—that they are better able to tolerate postoperative procedures such as chemotherapy. We bounce back more rapidly since the IV-C reduces the toxicity of the chemotherapy and radiation without compromising killing effects on cancer cells.

I returned home with three-fourths of my left lung floating in a preservative-filled lab jar somewhere at University Hospital. I escaped confinement after just five days rather than the ten days that Dr. Sen expected. That did not mean I felt okay—far from it.

I have an exceptionally high tolerance for pain, given my history of eight rib fractures, a broken sternum, a broken back, a broken leg, a broken hand, two broken arms, and a broken nose—nearly twenty fractures populating the geology of this Humpty-Dumpty. Pain and I are old friends. But the chest pain that I felt following lung surgery was beyond anything I had ever experienced. Tubes hung from every part of my body: an arterial line, a venous line, an oxygen tube in my nose, and several drainage tubes under my left armpit. A needle in my lower back delivered titrated morphine when I self-administered, and periodically Jody did her nurse thing by injecting me with various medications such as Heparin, an anticoagulant used to prevent formation of blood clots.

I could barely rise from my bed and walk into the bathroom. Jody, of course, tried to intercede. I insisted that she means many things to me in this life, yet bedpan-tender will never become one of her duties. I repeated, *never*. I'm shitting and peeing by myself, no matter what, thank you.

At first it took me almost five minutes just to make the short journey, and I sat on the stool breathless, miserable, and feeling defeated. So, while waiting to overcome constipation from all the medications and medical procedures, sitting there with no place else to go, I decided upon my one-year postoperative goal: run with Harley for three miles without stopping. One year later, I would run four miles nonstop. Then I would run three miles in under thirty minutes. These became my goals, and I intended to achieve them.

Late May 2010, a hospice in Denver, Colorado

I have been hospitalized nine times in the last seventeen months. I have had frequent episodes of weakness, nausea, and lack of appetite. I have watched my muscles deteriorate, losing mass and firmness. My skin and eyes have turned various shades of yellow, my skin an intense signal flag for jaundice. I have undergone numerous medical procedures during my hospital stays: aspirating built-up fluids in a large liver cyst, anticancer drugs injected directly into blood vessels feeding cancerous tumors, and even proton beam therapy, a procedure right out of a *Star Trek* movie: "Beam me up, Scotty." Each hospitalization has taken more out of me. I have waved the yellow flag and accepted my fate. I have submitted myself to hospice care, which is the first significant step toward what enlightened people call a good death.

Hospice comes from a Latin word hospitium, meaning guesthouse, historically describing a place of shelter for travelers who are weary or sick or both. Today the word stands for a special brand of care for patients with life-limiting illnesses, their families, and their caregivers. Hospice care emphasizes physical, emotional, and spiritual comfort for patients when curative treatment has been unsuccessful or is no longer preferred. This palliative approach to optimum patient comfort can be provided at home but is also available in long-term care and hospice inpatient facilities. As I mentioned earlier, I have chosen the latter alternative for my final weeks or days at the Denver Hospice, located in the Lowry neighborhood of east Denver. To receive Medicare payments for hospice, patients must be declared to have six months or less to live. Dr. Sen has made such a declaration about my deteriorating situation.

"How are you, Daddy?"

My sweet Kalinda bounces into my room, excited and full of energy. She is dark-complexioned, tall and full-figured like my amazing grandmother. She barely resembles my first wife Janice, who I have occasionally seen in the twenty-eight years since we divorced. Janice raised Kalinda, but I've stayed closed and contributed my share in alimony and school payments.

Kalinda is almost thirty now, a social worker based in Kansas City. She is passing through Denver on a short vacation trip to the Arapahoe Basin Ski Area for several days filled with snowboarding and more snowboarding. With a summit elevation of 13,050 feet, A-Basin is the last ski area to remain open following the regular season, sometimes keeping its slopes and lifts open until the first week of July. She's a chip off the old block, with fitness and adventure on the top of her list of priorities.

I give her a big, lingering hug. "Hey, honey, I'm glad you could stop by and see me. How are you?"

She sits on the edge of my bed, which has been littered with medical books and research studies about palliative care, part of my regimen to be as informed as possible about what is happening to me. "I'm terrific. We're very worried about you, though."

Her inclusive "we" I interpret to mean her younger half-sister Danielle, just finishing college and living with her mother Allyse, my second wife. Allyse left me after eighteen short months of marriage in the mid-1980s for her current husband, but this complex set of relationships has also found smooth waters of accommodation and co-parenting. "You and your sister don't need to worry."

Resorting to her former teenage habit of addressing me by my first name rather than Daddy, she says in a sharp tone, "You're in a hospice, Luke!"

"I know this is pretty much the end of the road, but I'm staying in control of the process." I look at her with a wink and reach for her hand, feminine yet strong. "Do you expect anything less from me?"

She takes my hand and settles at the end of the bed by crossing her legs Indian-style. "You look—pretty good."

"Now don't BS me. I know you mean well, but I look like a cartoon version of myself, swollen and painted yellow. All I need now is a yellow submarine."

She says, "You do look kind of yellowish. Is there anything they can do?"

"They're doing a terrific job of managing my pain and discomforts. That's their thing here."

She closes her eyes as if trying to hold back tears. "What can I do to help?"

"You're doing it right now. It means so much to me just to see you again. You're my favorite track star, you know." I am referring to a past chapter when Kalinda was a Missouri state champion in the 400-meter dash. She was fast and amazing, especially in the opinion of her dad. "Are you staying in shape?"

"Of course, Luke—" Her eyes become moist, and she turns away from me to rub away tears. "I don't want you to leave us, Daddy."

"I'm a survivor, always have been. Do you know what it means to be a survivor?"

She looks momentarily exasperated. "I'm your daughter and have watched you do all those dangerous stunts—"

"They were experiments!"

There comes a moment of silence. "Okay, experiments. I've seen you survive repeatedly. I think I understand what it means."

"A survivor is someone who continues to exist...someone who defies all odds and persists in the face of great trials."

She agrees finally. "You have lived through many trials, worrying all of us. But we've loved you no matter what. I've loved you no matter what." Tears flow freely from her eyes.

"I wish I could have been around more when you were growing up," I struggle to confess. "I'm grateful for the time we've had to be closer over the last several years."

She frowns. "I forgave you years ago. You didn't abandon me like a lot of divorced fathers. You came around."

"I'm sorry things didn't last for me with your mother," I say, stroking her hand.

"It's no longer an issue. You know I was mad at you at first. But you stayed involved in my youth sports and always tried to attend my track meets."

"I was so proud of my girl, the way she could fly down the track."

She looks at me a bit sheepishly. "I ran for you."

"I hope I didn't push too hard." Sudden sadness comes to me.

Nubile Nurse Heidi peeks around the open door to my room. "Will your daughter stay for lunch today, Dr. Luke?"

Kalinda turns toward Heidi. "I can't today. My boyfriend is waiting at a Starbucks. We have to be on our way to A-Basin before I-70 packs up with traffic." Then to me she says, "He has lots of work to do or he'd have stopped over to see you also."

"I understand," I say. Her boyfriend, Frank, is like so many when they might come face-to-face with a dying person. They want to stay away. I do understand.

Heidi says, "You let me know if you change your mind. Dr. Luke is one of our favorite guests." Without acknowledging Kalinda's understandable tears—they come regularly with the territory here—she smiles and rushes down the hall toward the dining room.

Turning again toward me, Kalinda begins to speak but hesitates.

"What are you thinking, hon?"

"I've always wondered if you've had much fun, as hard as you've pushed yourself."

"Fun is a matter of perception," I say, wiping her tears with my thumbs. "To survive this many years with the threat of cancer hanging over me has required a different point of view about life.

"Taking a vacation or bar-hopping never felt like fun to me. I have found fun in running with Jody and Harley. I have experienced joy in setting fitness goals and reaching them. Smelling early morning rain or watching cumulus clouds lumber across the evening sky—that's more fun than almost anything else I can imagine. Being close to others, having empathy for those who suffer, giving more than taking, feeling the sun on my cheeks—those are my ways of having fun."

She scoots up further on my bed and rests her head on my leg and I begin petting her silky, auburn hair like I did when she was a child. "Being with you now is all the fun I ask of this life."

"I can't stand to know you're dying." Her eyes fill again with tears.

"Then know I am living until the day I take my last breath. Like all the other days that have come before, that too will be a good day."

Chapter 10

SKYSCRAPER

*A*daptation is one of those words that has stuck with me. I have called upon this word to manage adversity. I have confronted more challenges to my well-being than most people ever do. My list of physical traumas and medical treatments can pack a two-inch-thick binder. From life-threatening sinus and ear infections in infancy to the recent loss of 70 percent of my left lung due to cancer, I have looked at adversity from all sides now. And I've learned a few things, perhaps best summed up by existential philosopher Friedrich Nietzsche: "That which does not kill us makes us stronger."

Interval training and persistency helped me reach my goal of running three miles nonstop one year after the removal of most of my left lung. I did this by getting out there and pushing myself beyond what most people would consider reasonable limits. I pushed through pain and lethargy. I fought depression and defeat. I kept my mental eye on the goal: successful completion of the twelfth lap of the running track at George Washington High School. Twelve laps equal three miles.

When physicians study the chest X-ray of someone who has had a lung removed, they see an empty cavity filled with fluid.

This is normal in a nonactive person. The X-ray of my lung cavity one-year post-op showed a cavity that had regenerated some lung tissue and had new vascularization. My air sacs—the alveoli—can never return, but the cavity filling with new tissue demonstrated a form of regeneration, of healthy adaptation to severe physical trauma. Air sacs in my right lung had doubled in size. Airways to and through my good lung had enlarged. My body had grown more efficient in processing oxygen, like how healthy people adapt over time to high altitudes.

Lung cancer had not killed me, and I had become stronger for it. I had adapted.

January 2009, Denver, Colorado

Republic Plaza commands the Denver skyline as the tallest skyscraper, a fifty-six-story behemoth rising 714 feet above the Mile High City. Completed in 1984, it stands in line as the 109th tallest building in the United States and the tallest building in Colorado, all fifty-six floors of it. The scale of this challenge, which someone like me who is afraid of heights does not underestimate, was not why I had chosen to climb it.

Republic Plaza is home to an American Lung Association annual fundraising event: Colorado's *Fight for Air Climb*. The fitness challenge occurs during the last Sunday in February, a fifty-six-story stair climb to the top of the building. As many as 2,400 fit people participate; they raise about five hundred thousand dollars for the American Lung Association in Colorado.

Do you see the superb irony of a one-lung man, a victim of lung cancer, climbing this skyscraper in symbolic tribute? But I added a hitch: I would climb on the outside of the building rather than using stairs—and without permission.

With fifty-four mountains in Colorado towering fourteen-thousand feet or more above sea level, you may be wondering why I did not choose to scale one of those purple mountain majesties or all of them, thereby admitting myself to the elite *Fourteener's Club*. That would have been quite an achievement—especially all fifty-four summits for a man with greatly diminished lung capacities.

Republic Plaza symbolized something no Rocky Mountain ever can: confinement of the human spirit. Office building workers everywhere know the feelings associated with artificial air, artificial light, and artificial control over their sense of freedom. Pay might be adequate. Sharing corporate identity has some merit. Job security means a lot. But modern technocratic society suppresses and limits interaction with nature. Buildings force unnatural interactions and sometimes foster the worst of human nature through corporate politics, blame games, and institutionalized deceitfulness. I had tasted my share of confinement in buildings and offices, and whenever an alternative became possible, I took the road less traveled. And for me, that made all the difference.

Jody had argued against this decision, as by now you might expect, especially given the delicate nature of my lung capacity and the toll that lung surgery had taken on my overall well-being. We had a brief but pointed discussion.

She had said, "You're going to climb Republic Plaza? That seems like a creative way to commit suicide."

"You know me and how I approach risk factors," I answered. "I'm committed to gradual desensitization of my agoraphobia and endurance and strength training until I reach the equivalent of able-bodied capacity."

"What's necessary to illegally climb a building with no climbing experience?"

"Preparation."

She had glared at me with fury in her eyes. "Have you considered the larger picture here?"

"Larger picture?"

"Yes, larger. Have you thought about the impact of your risky behavior on me and your daughters?"

She had made a salient point: the three most important women in my life had not been part of my deliberations and commitment to ascend the building. "I love all three of you more than anything. So, I will be deliberate in my preparations and as cautious as possible."

She threw a book she had been reading on the floor. "I get it that you believe taking risks keeps you around longer—"

"I believe it and I have proven it—at least to my satisfaction."

"But, get this…I have questioned whether you might be setting up a scenario for your suicide, perhaps unconsciously. Each stunt—or experiment, as you call them—presents escalating danger if you make a mistake."

I then walked over to her and held her shoulders to keep her focus on what I had to say. "I have made lots of mistakes, honey. The mistake I won't make is to fall to my death from Republic Plaza. This will be my final feat—and I will win."

"Your final feat? Is that a promise you can keep?"

I put my arm around her and walked her to our bed, where we sat. "This is it. My body won't tolerate much more stress. But

I'm very convinced that everything I've learned about the human body and risk taking will pay off this final time." I may be a risk-taker, but I could not allow my stubbornness to cost me a relationship with this remarkable woman.

She sighed and dropped her head on my shoulder. "Then I'm going to be involved in every step of preparation—strength training, aerobic fitness, diet, planning, and technology—everything. Got it?"

"Of course. I welcome your support."

"And I will be at the top of Republic Plaza when you get there."

"We risk incarceration."

"Do you think I give a damn? If you don't succeed and fall, then nothing else that follows is going to make me feel worse. If you succeed, then going to jail is a very temporary inconvenience."

It hadn't happened often. I have felt emotions at very deep levels, but I rarely displayed them, especially the emotions connected to tears, whether sadness, loneliness, or even elation. I had learned to suppress those feelings at St. Mark's. But this moment brought me to tears and Jody held me in her arms, understanding the emotional release that her tacit permission had given me. She had granted me her okay to climb a building, and she had given her permission for me to be me—and I know of no greater gift bestowed by one human upon another.

So, it had ended well, and Jody fulfilled her commitment to support and coach me for the climb of my life. She occupied her focus on my physical preparations, while I took care of the mental and technological aspects. According to her wishes, I consulted with her about every decision.

We began each day with a run through Washington Park. The cold January air was not a great idea for my lungs—lung—but I took a precautionary step of wearing a surgical mask to warm the air before it filled my lung. I was not as fast as her anymore, and I did not try to compete, but she always ran just slightly faster than my legs wanted to run, thus building up more cardiovascular reserves than I believed possible.

That was just the start of the typical training day. Next, I undertook step-ups on a workout bench while carrying a twenty-pound pack of weights on my back. She insisted that I perform five hundred repetitions on the twenty-two-inch bench as fast as possible. She refused to be satisfied with my performance until I could execute five hundred reps in ten minutes. This regimen replicated a vertical distance of at least eight-hundred feet, more than enough to simulate the climbing distance from street level to the building roof. When I undertook this grueling routine, I would always look up while imagining the roof's lip above the highest floor of the building, my destination. I would repeat to myself, "There's your goal, Luke. It's coming closer with each step—closer with each step—closer with each step."

Then, while she worked her shift at the hospital, I would spend two hours each afternoon training with weights, concentrating on my triceps and forearms, the primary load-bearing muscles needed for climbing. I stayed away from bench presses and push-ups because my lung removal surgery—the pneumonectomy—required that several ribs had to be broken, but even so I had to grit my teeth through significant pain.

It did not kill me, and it made me stronger.

Jody focused on our diet with obsession for details. She increased our fiber intake to forty grams a day for her and eighty grams a day for me. This she accomplished with natural bran cereals, beans, apples, broccoli, dried fruit, and brown rice. She made sure that 70 to 80 percent of our protein intake came from plant sources such as tofu, soy products, nuts, seeds, and whole grains. The rest of our protein intake came from fish high in Omega-3 fatty acid such as salmon, halibut, swordfish, and tuna. This polyunsaturated fatty acid has shown promise in reducing inflammation and pain, two of my daily battles.

Instead of eating three squares every day, we ate six or more smaller feedings. This provided better regulation of our blood sugar levels and allowed for enhanced absorption of nutrients. This, along with lots of fiber, reduced transit time from mouth to stool while maintaining a healthier digestive system and diminishing the odds that I might get sick with a cold or the flu. She also made sure that we supplemented our diet with vitamins C, D, B-complex, and E.

With her job managed to perfection, I focused on desensitizing myself from fear of heights. I began by taking an elevator to the top floor of Republic Plaza, dressed as a typical businessman, and then observing the cityscape from this lofty height. Deep breathing helped me shift from feelings of fear to those of marvel for the beauty in the Denver skyline. Then at street-level I would look up the skyscraper one floor at a time while imagining myself climbing up the rails used for window washing that run vertical with the building. Those rails promised a lifeline to the top. Sometimes I would take a total of thirty minutes to study every step up I would take, becoming familiar with the building surfaces and unique architectural characteristics. I visited other nearby skyscrapers and when possible would look at Republic Plaza from the perspective of high altitude, becoming intimately familiar with the city skyline from that perspective. Over time, fear transitioned into a sense of control—that the soaring building and my ascent were not threats but allies in my *Mission Impossible*.

Finally, I collaborated with two of my engineering buddies, both professors from the Colorado School of Mines, to design spring-loaded cams for my feet and hands. These climbing devices could ride up the surface of the window washing rails. We undertook a reconnaissance of the building late one night to measure the rails with calipers, so the cams would fit the rails perfectly. The ingenious spring-loaded cams could move up as determined by movement of my feet and hands then lock into place until released for the next movement upward. Again, late one night about one week before my building ascent, we tested the climbing devices by my ascending about fifty feet. Fortunately, the building guard and cruising police had not seen this assault on the building, and the devices worked exactly as my engineering friends had designed them.

Sunday, February 15, 2009, Republic Plaza, downtown Denver, Colorado

At almost noon on a calm and sunny day in mid-February, I had reached the fourteenth floor before anyone of any consequence had noticed. My support team had shrunken to the size of ants below. I was fourteen minutes into the climb. Curious faces had begun staring at me from office windows. A crowd had gathered on the street below. Police cars had also started arriving. I was in my flow zone, deliberately lifting one foot, then one hand, then the other foot, and then the other hand. I had become a machine focused on my goal. Jody had already snuck onto the roof above, aware that she would soon be joined by authorities and eventually by the Denver police. I had become a syncopated organism feeling much less fear than I imagined I might.

I was becoming Republic Plaza, my atoms melding into the skyscraper. My single lung expanded with the cleaner air above the city. Twenty floors above street-level. Then thirty. I hesitated at the thirty-fifth floor to survey my city, sensing the majesty of human creativity and artistry in so many buildings. Images of buildings behind me, reflected in window glass, represented my misty dreams about human possibilities and achievements. Far below were the restaurants that Jody and I loved, especially the Mercury Café, a throwback to the sixties, where an organic and wholesome meal would follow my triumphant success (assuming we were not incarcerated overnight). I studied the traffic jams typical of this time of day and wondered how many of those cars included smokers sucking on cigarettes. Everyone has two lungs, but I had taken advantage of the single lung that God had left me. I was healthier than most of those life-insured bodies, although I could never get life insurance. Around the thirty-eighth floor, curious office workers stared and pointed at me, and in one impetuous moment I allowed myself the additional risk of smiling and waving back. At the thirty-ninth floor, I saw another group of office workers, also smiling and waving. One of the workers looked familiar, although I could not place his face or physique, but I waved again at that huddle of curious onlookers. They also smiled and waved back, perhaps recognizing the ironies in my courage, my mastery over fear of high places. And I continued my journey upward: the fortieth floor, then the fiftieth—just six floors between me and salvation. And then the cam in my left hand slipped. My body sweat had streamed down my forearm and into the climbing device, but I did not panic. I stopped again and considered all the gifts of my life in that instant, my determination, the women I have loved and who have loved me, my intense appreciation of nature, and my choices that have assured a career with maximum separation from a command-and-control world. And then I continued upward: floors fifty-one, fifty-two, fifty-three, and fifty-four. I looked across the cityscape toward the mountains, sensing how temporary this moment in time, how unrepeatable. And I continued pushing myself one floor more, then two floors, until I reached over the lip of the roof and pulled myself onto its surface exactly fifty minutes after I had begun my ascent.

Building security and two police officers escorted Jody and me to street-level. As we exited the building, a gaggle of news reporters intercepted us. It appeared that we had become that night's lead story. We had the great good fortune of being escorted by Sgt. Fred Samuels, a Denver police officer whom I have known for years. We had lifted weights together at 24-Hour Fitness where I sometimes worked out. Fred had already heaped a pile of crap on us, but he also had a wry smile, understanding the humor embedded in a guy with one lung climbing a building where annually they would raise money to support lung cancer research. Instead of pushing through the crush of reporters, he stopped and allowed me to answer questions.

The ABC affiliate reporter took the first shot. The young male in a frumpy white dress shirt asked, "Why did you climb the building? What did you expect to accomplish?"

I looked at him with my typical serious expression. "I am a lung cancer survivor, and I believe this is another way to bring attention to the disease. The *Fight for Air Climb* will occur inside Republic Plaza nine days from today. I undertook this demonstration out of respect and appreciation for building management and tenants who annually support the American Lung Association and this important fundraiser. My intention is to encourage more of the community to get behind the fundraiser and support the climbers."

"Didn't you put yourself and innocent pedestrians in grave danger with such a stunt?"

"I believe part of the point is that some of your viewers watching this report put themselves in far greater danger by smoking cigarettes, eating high-fat diets, and living sedentary lifestyles."

"What does a stunt like this accomplish except to invite copycats?"

"I managed all the risk factors, preparing for many weeks. This was not an impulsive stunt but a carefully planned demonstration of our innate capabilities to achieve more than we believe possible—if each of us embraces wellness principles."

A television reporter with another station continued the interrogation. "Why did you get lung cancer? Are you a smoker?"

"Cancer is a mysterious disease that can strike anyone, anytime. But we can manage risks by not smoking and staying fit. My doctors believe that I have had four bouts of cancer since childhood, now spanning more than fifty-five years, because of overexposure to X-ray radiation when I was an infant—"

"You've never smoked?"

"Never. And I have doctorates in exercise physiology and sports psychology, so fitness has been my way of life since childhood. Through my professional work, I am dedicated to helping heart attack victims recover and thrive."

The reporter appeared momentarily dumbfounded, so another young female reporter with a radio station shoved a microphone in my face. "Weren't you terrified of falling?"

"I used to be frightened of heights, but I've worked through my fears. I have come to love what I once feared most. That is my definition of happiness."

A man unfamiliar to me stepped forward. He had a towering stature with a full head of silver hair, obviously fit for his age, a leader by his bearing. "My name is Justin Wharton. I am chairman of the American Lung Association in Denver and the board's major gift co-chair. I have a pertinent announcement if you will please permit me to make a statement."

The expanding group of reporters and spectators pushed closer to hear what he had to say. He reached over and gently grabbed my arm, pulling me closer to him. He then kept his hand on my right shoulder. "We have not met this man before, but he has just had a substantial impact on our annual fundraiser."

Speaking both to me and to the reporters, he continued, "Are you aware that this building has a major tenant occupying six floors, from floor thirty-seven to forty-two?"

I thought about it, considering that this research probably should also have been part of my feat preparation, but I didn't have a clue. "No, I do not."

"The management of this company has tacitly supported our *Fight for Air Climb* by encouraging their employees to participate, but up to this point they have provided nominal financial support for our fundraiser. That is, until today."

Wharton looked pleased and proud as he paused a moment for dramatic effect. "The CEO of this respected Republic Plaza tenant, a company that is one of the pillars of Denver's growing high-tech industry, has just informed me about a matching grant. For every dollar raised by more than 2,500 stair climbers we have signed up for our annual stair climb, the company has agreed to match donations, dollar-for-dollar."

Again, he paused for theatrical impact. "Ladies and gentlemen, this generous grant to support the American Lung Association and our programs to fight lung diseases has a value of over half a million dollars." The crowd reacted with spontaneous applause and cheers. Looking at me, he added, "And for the courage and commitment you've demonstrated today, I want to thank you." I nodded in reply.

While holding a microphone bearing the Fox network logo, a professionally dressed African-American reporter stepped forward. "Which company is making the grant?"

Wharton seemed to grow even taller than his six-foot, two-inch stature, proud and grateful. "This unprecedented donation has been made by software developer Strategic Horizons and its CEO, Bill Smith."

I was thunderstruck by this news. Bill Smith had once been my least favorite cardiac rehabilitation patient, a total asshole as I remembered him, the same very ill man who had refused to accept the necessity for him to make drastic lifestyle changes following his myocardial infarction. In my mind, I then recalled the setting of our heart-to-heart conversation in the gardens outside the hospital and his tearful confession of grief—that tender cathartic moment when all the pretenses and game-playing dissolved between two ambitious and competitive men.

Wharton looked behind him at a group of techies who had gathered adjacent to the building exit. "Mr. Smith?"

I was shocked again as a thin, fit, and vigorous man stepped forward. Bill Smith had lost his beer gut; his complexion looked ruddy and healthy; his stride appeared more confident. He stood next to me on my left with Wharton on my right. He, too, placed a hand on my shoulder.

"I am Bill Smith, founder and CEO of Strategic Horizons," he began. Then nodding at me, he continued, "This man saved my life. I was a smoker for thirty-five years, overweight, and sedentary. I paid the price ten years ago by almost dying from a heart attack—"

"How did he whip you into shape?" interrupted the Fox reporter. Laughter followed from the crowd.

"Dr. Luke made me aware of the depth of our capacities as mortal humans. He taught me how I could overcome resistance to change, beat my tobacco and food addictions, and choose well-being over illness—how to take responsibility for my health. He didn't nag or behave like a bossy high school gym coach. He led by example, and those of you who witnessed what he accomplished here today now understand what I mean." He looked at me and reached to shake my hand, "Thank you, Dr. Luke, for saving my life." I could not find the words to answer, taking his hand and nodding instead.

Enthusiastic applause and cheers reverberated from the majestic skyscrapers that surrounded us. I noticed that Jody's eyes had filled with tears, not of sadness but of joy.

… Chapter 11

FIERCE

October 2009, at home, Denver, Colorado

Jody had fallen back to sleep, her body turned away from me and curled up, like a beautiful model in calm repose, sandy hair covering most of her face. I studied her contours in that gray light, admiring the soft luster of her skin and her well-proportioned musculature, sinewy and defined, and even though she had excused me for my lapse, I still felt in the wrong for my failure to be present and attentive during our lovemaking.

We had awoken an hour earlier to a stormy Sunday morning with rain pattering the roof, the type of lazy weekend day that invites you to sleep for an extra hour or two. But she woke up quickly, issuing soft sighs and a whimper she reserved just for me. It was her way of telling me that she wanted to make love. I concluded that she must have had an early morning sexual dream that propelled her from deep slumber to high passion in a matter of moments.

She had been more aggressive than usual, kissing, grabbing and stroking. I rolled her on top and allowed her to escort me into her, and I let her be the conductor of a syncopated concert. I was there but I wasn't, and she sensed this.

Maybe my reaction had been a consequence of my own fitful and troubling dreams earlier that morning, which involved my falling into a dark well with no bottom. Perhaps inspired by her surprising eagerness so early, I also became excited and more insistent, but I was no longer with her emotionally. My body was below her; my head was someplace else, making my actions automatic and detached. I have never been that kind of distracted lover.

I disregarded her entreaties to be with her— "Please come back to me, Luke"— hearing her ask me to recouple but continuing with disconnected, mechanical motions. I had been sexually aroused, yes. And inspired by lust. But I was also angry—not at my sweet, self-sacrificing Jody, but at my status in the battle for life.

I was angry at medical ignorance that had subjected an infant to high doses of X-ray radiation to treat a simple sinus infection. I was pissed that an unfiltered overdose of radiation had wrecked my body's protective system, which stops unwarranted cell division. I was irritated at the apparent inadequacy of my regimen of intense physical fitness and careful diet and my decades of study to learn the secrets about maintaining healthful functioning of the human body. I was enraged over my coarse memories of Sarge, that asshole psychopath at St. Mark's, who had murdered three puppies and enjoyed it. I was livid at obesity and cigarette addiction and cheesy nachos and mindless television sit-coms, all conspiring to rob many Americans of their health and vitality. I was angry at myself for failing to eradicate cancer from my body. Most of all, in those hasty minutes of hypercharged passion with Jody, I was infuriated with God for punishing me even though I had dedicated my life to diligent work for health and wellness and prayer to Him.

Why was He letting me down? What lesson was I supposed to learn that I missed, dear sweet Lord?

We came together, although I knew Jody's orgasmic gasp was a mixture of pleasure and concern, and she then held me close with her arms and legs wrapped tightly around me, stroking my back and urging me to calm down.

"Please forgive me, hon," I said, panting from exertion.

She embraced me with greater force and said, "I know you're not angry at me or disconnected because that's your preference. I know that." Then she pushed me back, so I could see her bedroom eyes and consider the heart of a human being with whom I had surrendered everything. "I know you're mad at your illness and the uncertainties of tomorrow. Let's just not make love again when you feel so distracted by other things."

"I feel like I'm failing."

"Don't ever think that again, Luke. You have accomplished more in the name of wellness and managed your diseases better than anyone I've ever known. And I'm a nurse, so I have a lot of experience with people and suffering." She kissed me quickly all over my face as I capitulated to her tender mercies. "I am so proud of you."

I must admit that then I cried, which I have not done so shamelessly without inhibition in years or even decades. I cannot remember when. She held me until she fell back to sleep, rain pummeling the roof of our home with mesmerizing white noise. I am sure she fell back to sleep from exhaustion, physical and emotional. I marveled at the burdens she carried without complaining too much.

So, then I rested on the king-size bed, numb from the release of many uncensored emotions, guilt washing over me for my self-centeredness. To be fully candid, I wasn't merely angry at all the narratives and storylines from my past life that you already understand. One other critical piece of information remained unspoken: I had learned two days earlier that cancer had invaded my liver, and I had not told Jody, my daughters, or anyone else. I had held the burden close for too long.

Most of us wonder what it will be like to grow old, but few give this inevitable direction of our life course any more conscious deliberation than necessary, especially when we are young and vital and much of our adult lives span out before us. I believe that for many of us in youth we secretly harbor a childish fantasy or perhaps an unexamined wish that old age will pass us by. *Magical thinking.* We cannot envision or accept our much older selves, so we don't give the processes and consequences of aging more consideration than necessary. Some of us are guilty of teasing old people or at least deriding them in our innermost thoughts. Sometimes ageism creeps into our conversations with our young peers. Phrases such as "that old geezer…" or "that old crone…" begin a few adolescent sentences concerned with the subject of old age. We believe in our deepest prejudices and stereotypes that aged humans are from a different species than our own, thus legitimate targets for objectification, derision, and marginalization. Dr. Robert Butler, the brilliant physician who coined the word "ageism," described the source of this prejudice as "the fearsome thought of growing old."

My most profound encounter with aging occurred during my teen years when my beloved grandmother started slipping away. In the span of a few months, she had transformed from a robust middle-aged woman into someone becoming decrepit and cognitively slower. A bright, ever-present twinkle in her sky-blue eyes had begun to dull, a sense of increasing vacancy in the thoughts behind those eyes. This process had alarmed me because her vigor and confidence had buoyed me through childhood and my early teen years, especially during the difficult time of my recuperation and recovery from neurogenic sarcoma and the months of weakness and disillusionment that followed.

She always told me to meet life head on, never to retreat or withdraw, but in her waning months she had begun to withdraw. It was as if what they tell us about dying people is true: they spend part of their final days somewhere else, in another realm or dimension, preparing to leave permanently for the other side of life. They are halfway in this dimension and halfway in another.

My concluding visit with her became a final gift in that she helped me understand what an old and dying person believes about the conclusion of life—in this case, a remarkable woman with great intelligence and extraordinary accomplishments. Holding her hand and speaking softly, I asked her if she had anything else she wanted to do.

She remained quiet for a long time, lying serenely in a beautiful and snuggly bed, covered with quilts she had stitched by hand and fluffy pillows in their antique lace pillowcases. This alarmed me: that she did not hear me or perhaps failed to understand my question.

Then she spoke with clarity. "I have not traveled as much as I might have," she said. "I have a few things that I planned to do and did not, such as write one more organic foods cookbook. But what I have not accomplished does not matter now. What is done is done. What hasn't been accomplished did not need to be. My life is complete and perfect as it has been." She seemed to drift off again.

In the lull, I looked around her bedroom and its showcase of wisdom, the well-crafted antiques, the stacked volumes of medicinal books, the bookshelves brimming with brown and green glass bottles harboring unknown potions and nutritional supplements. For the first time, I noticed a framed quotation, rendered in an old-style typeface. Florida Scott-Maxwell, an analytical psychologist who had studied under Carl Jung in the mid-twentieth century, an intellect I had learned of in college, expressed how I was beginning to understand acceptance of life's rough edges and incomplete stories:

You need to claim the events in your life to make yourself yours. When you truly possess all you have been and done, which may take some time, you are fierce with reality.

I then tried to bring her back to me again. "But, Grams, don't you wish you had more time to write that cookbook?"

Her eyes snapped open with blue intensity. "Luke, my sugarplum, when I reflect upon my life I really do not find a laundry list of unfinished business. I do not have a mental notebook filled with things I must do. I have done them. This is a contentment that aging can bring to an old soul. You'll understand someday." She floated away again, a peaceful vibe flowing with her wake, her fluffy white hair perfectly in place, her head barely denting a pillow, and her walnut-brown complexion lined with a lifetime of stories like mine would become many years later.

That was the last time I saw her alive, making me forever mindful of her absolute acquiescence to the script of her life. In the end, maybe peace comes. Maybe there is reconciliation before our final rest.

"Last time we met I shared that you have tumors in your liver," said Dr. Sen, who, with his calm composure, had mastered the art of delivering shocking news. "The follow-up CAT scan has confirmed the size and position of them. The largest mass is in the central section of your chest, Luke."

"Them?"

Dr. Sen shifted in his executive chair and gazed at Jody and me with disquiet in his expression. "Enumerable."

Jody said, "How many is *enumerable*, doctor?"

"Dozens. We know for certain that Luke's liver is much larger than normal and quite diseased."

Continuing her interrogation as Nurse Jody, she asked, "What is your recommended treatment plan?"

"The large mass I mentioned is the size of a tennis ball, and we propose to aspirate that tumor to relieve some pressure and the buildup of fluids. We think that will reduce the bilirubin problem that is contributing to Luke's recent jaundice and lethargy. It's also a factor in the odd taste in his mouth and his itchiness. I think we can make some or all of that go away for now."

I heard the news but flipped into a detached scientific mode, ticking off in my mind all the functions served by our livers that I could recall. The liver is a so-called "vital organ" for good reason, even though this biochemistry lab performs its vital functions without our necessarily being aware of them. We feel our hearts beat and know that a consistent, chest-thumping tick-tock is vital for survival; we feel our lungs expand and contract and know that breathing is immediate and vital. But our livers are more enigmatic.

The liver, a diminutive three-pound organ in a man my size, performs over five hundred different biochemical functions outside of conscious awareness. The organ's major achievements include bile production, which promotes absorption of fats from the gastrointestinal tract; excretion of cholesterol, hormones, and drugs; metabolism of proteins and carbohydrates; storage of glycogen, vitamins, and minerals; synthesis of plasma proteins, such as albumin; synthesis of blood clotting factors; the recycling of red blood cells so new cells can then be created; and maintenance of a stable concentration of blood glucose, which helps us sustain more consistent physical energy throughout the day...

"Luke, are you hearing what Dr. Sen is saying?" Jody looked at me with an insistent, clinical demeanor.

"Yes. Forgive me. I was just recalling some of the details of why the liver is vital for survival." I then directed my comments to the doctor. "Dr. Sen, I know liver hepatocytes have the unique capacity to reproduce in response to injuries. In fact, liver regeneration can occur after surgical removal of a portion of the liver or after blunt-impact traumas. Is that correct?"

Jody jumped onto my train of thought. "Yes, doctor, is it possible to surgically remove the diseased tissue in Luke's liver and allow regeneration of remaining healthy tissue?"

Mirroring Jody's clinical demeanor, Dr. Sen said, "Although the liver's ability to repair itself is wondrous, repetitive assaults, such as those imposed by metastasizing malignancies, can contradict possibilities of healthy regeneration. Tumors have distributed throughout the left and right lobes of Luke's liver, negating the potential value of surgical removal of diseased tissue and hope for regeneration." He appeared genuinely concerned and sympathetic, not just coldly clinical. "I am so sorry."

Jody persisted. "What about chemoembolization?"

My anger, lurking on the sidelines, returned to the game with vengeance. "Jody, you know that I *will not* submit to chemotherapy! The one thing that has kept me alive all these years is my robust immune system, and chemo wipes out immunity. They just about have to kill you to keep you alive with that stuff. Chemo will make me a sitting duck for pneumonia and other infectious diseases known to attack compromised immune systems—"

"Hon, I know how you feel about chemo. But chemoembolization targets only the tumors, with medication injected directly through a catheter. Is that right, doctor?"

Hardheaded as I could be, I interrupted. "Why would you inject yourself with a poison that goes through your entire body to maybe kill an isolated tumor? How logical is that, Nurse Jody?"

Dr. Sen said, "Yes, Jody, for this treatment we mix chemotherapy drugs with particles called microspheres, which block the flow of blood to the tumor. The tumor no longer has the oxygen and nutrients it needs to grow—"

"And it's more effective than traditional chemo?" Jody pressed.

"Yes, chemoembolization allows for higher doses of drugs to be targeted directly to the cancerous tissue for a longer period, without exposing the entire body to the nasty invasiveness of the drugs. The procedure diminishes classic chemo side effects such as nausea, vomiting, and loss of appetite."

I felt furious about being bushwhacked. "I *will not undergo chemo* ... of any kind!"

Dr. Sen leaned forward, placing both hands on his desk. "It is okay, Luke. I understand. You are not a candidate for chemoembolization. Your disease is too advanced. You have too many tumors, in addition to your long history with other types of cancer as well."

Jody's eyes filled with tears and I felt regretful for my temper tantrum. It seemed that anger had become the theme of my life. She asked, "What about a liver transplant—"

"Yes, Dr. Sen, you said this cancer appears confined to my liver. And I have an excellent immune system. I never get sick with the flu, colds, or other contagious illnesses. I just grow tumors."

"One of the primary criteria for transplants is that the patient has been free of active cancer growth systemically for five years. You had prostate cancer about a year ago—"

"But the urologist declared my prostate cancer to be fully in remission, without any residual signs of disease. The radioactive seed implants cured me!"

"Luke, I'm so sorry, but you're not a viable transplant candidate. You'll never be approved for this kind of aggressive treatment and placed on an organ donor waiting list."

Placing her head in her hands, Jody openly sobbed, and I reached for her to hold and comfort her. Nurse Jody no more, she became my sweetheart, my spiritual partner, the person I pledged to protect, the best parts of my life for many years. Dr. Sen remained silent, appearing to read a memo. Jody glanced at me, her eyes and nose cherry red. "What do we do now, Luke?"

"Cancer will not deter me any more than I'm willing to let it. It may win the war, but I'm going to win every battle until the end. I am ready for a long run in Washington Park. How about you?"

Chapter 12

REDEMPTION

July 2010, a hospice in Denver, Colorado

"What are you doing, Dr. Luke?" asks Helen, nurse supervisor at Denver Hospice, charging into my room.

With my face and chest pressed to the carpet, I am in a prone position, my hands flat on the floor and on either side of me. I glance up at her. "I have been trying to do a few push-ups."

"Is that a good idea?"

"Helen, it doesn't matter if it's a good idea. I used to rip off five hundred push-ups in fifteen minutes. Today I can barely get up to ten."

She looks exasperated but sympathetic. I know her expressions well. "I don't want you to hurt yourself—"

"Really? What difference would that make now? My body is about as broken down as it can be to keep me alive. I just want to test myself one more time."

"Maybe testing yourself this way won't help you feel better?"

With effort, I push myself up and into a sitting position. "I've always tested and measured myself. That's what exercise physiologists and sports psychologists do. But I understand your point—"

"I want to be sure that our favorite guest has many good days here." She smiles, more with sympathy than exasperation.

"I'm finished with this test. I didn't pass with flying colors. But I did my best, and that's all I ever asked of my rehab patients."

"Come on, let me help you." She reaches for my hands and then steps back slowly as I rise to my feet, feeling wobbly and weak. Her strength is remarkable. I'm delighted that the nurse supervisor also shares my passion for fitness.

"Dr. Luke, I dropped in to suggest that you swing by Charlie's room. He's fading pretty fast, and he asked to speak with you." I nod affirmatively, she turns, and I follow her to the other end of the hospice. We chatter about nonsensical things: the lunch menu, a garden party tonight for those able to leave their rooms, the political campaign for Denver's mayoral office.

Filled with morning light from windows facing east, Charlie's room is breathing with the vivid colors of at least five flower bouquets. He is resting in his bed at a forty-five-degree angle. His frail body has been connected to a medical ventilator through intubation by way of a tracheotomy. This has been done for his comfort more than to prolong his life. Like me, he has signed orders not to resuscitate when one of his vital organs fails.

Lisping today even more like a sodden asthmatic, he speaks barely above a whisper. "You...well...today?"

"As much as can be expected, Charlie. I knocked off nine push-ups. Not bad for a guy who once could do five hundred—"

"Push-ups...not...important," he wheezes back.

"I know. I know. I just can't easily break old habits."

"I'm...ready...to...suit...up. Old...habit."

He seems to be looking through me. "Do you mean you're ready to suit up for a basketball game?"

"Big...game."

"Is all your team there?"

"Yes...whole team. I...want you...too?"

"You want me to be on your team?"

"Yes."

I glance over at Helen, who has been busy checking his vital signs and reviewing his chart. She is behind Charlie's head so he cannot see her, and she frowns and shakes her head back and forth. "Charlie wants me on his team. I'm honored." Speaking to him, I answer, "Count me in as number two. I used to be a pretty good shooting guard in my time."

Charlie smiles again. "You...get...better with...good coach."

"And I have always known how to pick my coaches well. Rock Chalk, Jayhawk!"

With my recitation of the famous University of Kansas chant, he grins and lifts his right arm, pointing his index finger at something only he can see. "Rock...Chalk...everyone."

"Yes, I am sure they are. It is time for the big game, isn't it?"

He drops his arm and closes his eyes, a satisfied look on his sunken, gray face, and he drifts into unconsciousness. Helen checks his vital signs again and nods for me to leave the room with her.

Outside his room, she puts her hand on my arm. "Not long now," she says. "His pulse is very weak. I think his time has come. We've called his children so they can get here as soon as possible. Do you know why he picked you?"

"Picked me?"

"You are the right confidant for him now. You understand his athletic side. You make him feel complete about that part of his life."

"I expected him to survive me."

"We just never know, Luke." Helen escorts me down the hallway in the direction of my room.

Heidi rushes by us, aiming toward Charlie's room. "Dr. Luke, you have another visitor."

Helen gives my arm a squeeze and strides off to attend other duties as I turn into the doorway of my room. Sitting in a sunbeam in a stately chair next to my bed is my youngest daughter, Danielle; she is reading a book that is resting on her lap. We have always called her Danni. She is shorter than my daughter Kalinda, with dark reddish hair, a white complexion like ivory, and amber-brown eyes framed by long black eyelashes. She is striking in her natural simplicity, a daughter who takes after my second wife Allyse, herself a throwback to the sixties, an authentic Earth-Mama mama. "Hello, Father."

Danni is formal with me, a bit more restrained than her half-sister, probably because we were not together as a family after she started elementary school. I've tried to stay close through customary visits to her home in Colorado Springs, but she hasn't bonded with me as much as my more athletic daughter. "It's so good to see you." I move toward her, she stands, and we share a quick hug. I kiss her on her cheek then sit on the edge of my bed; she settles again in the Victorian-style bedside chair.

She surveys me from head to foot. "You look tired."

"Yes, I am. I just visited with one of my fellow hospice inmates. He doesn't have much time. Charlie went to KU."

"Rock chalk, Jayhawk," she says with noticeable sarcasm. A graduate of the University of Colorado, she has always been a diehard Buffalos fan. That has been a wellspring for much cajoling and teasing over the years.

"Is your mother doing well?"

"Mother is great. She works part-time for Whole Foods on Hampden in the gift department. She's traveling overseas a lot. She's checking off many items on her bucket list." Danni places the open book back on her knees. I can see it is a bible.

"That's great news. You give her my best, will you?"

"Yes, I will. She has expressed grave concern about your poor health but just can't bring herself to visit you here. You know?"

"Allyse always got creepy around sick people and hospitals, given her obsessions with health foods, wellness programs, alternative medicine—"

"She still cares about you. Don't read anything into her not coming for a visit."

I lean forward and give my hand to her. "I know, honey. I have no expectations for her, other than a long and healthy life and many good times with you and your half-sister. Are you all getting along okay?"

She takes my hand and smiles softly. "Mother loves Kalinda and so do I. We're connected as a family, and we get together when possible—about every two months. Jody and you have been welcome."

"I regret now that we did not take Allyse up on one of her invitations for a Sunday dinner together. I've been focused elsewhere and busy. I'm sorry."

Danni shakes her head. "You don't need to apologize. I'm not angry. Mother isn't either. We've often prayed together for your recovery."

I look at the book in her lap, a velvet green ribbon marks a page of importance. I shrug and grin. "You can see that your prayers have not been answered this time."

She squeezes my hand; her eyes become moist. "That's partly why I'm here now. Are you a Christian, Father?"

"Please, honey, call me Dad or Luke. You know that I'm a very spiritual person—have been all my life. I shared with you a long time ago that I am not committed to a specific dogma. My early experiences with a Christian church—the one at St. Mark's—made me suspicious of organized religion."

"I remember. But I worry about your salvation. You know that Jesus Christ is the only way to eternal life."

I can see genuine concern sweeping across her round and innocent face. "I know that Christians believe this. I don't begrudge their faith. I also believe in a spiritual force greater than one religion. I have always thought of myself as a servant of God. He has helped me get through some tough times; yet my life has been filled with many blessings—including you."

She shifts from the chair to my bed, wrapping her arm around me while still clinging to the bible. I put my arm around her. "But Jesus is the way, the truth, and the life. You cannot be with our Father but through Him. Will you be born again?" I shake my head negatively. "For me?"

I rest my head on hers, feeling a surge of warmth from this intense and well-meaning daughter. "Nothing is more important to me now than loving my family, helping others when I can, sharing, and listening. I have always known that I need God, and I have always needed you. So, yes, for you, Danni, I will become a born-again Christian. You lead the way, honey."

She pulls the bible closer and grasps it with both hands, reading from a page she has marked: "Now there was a Pharisee, a man named Nicodemus who was a member of the Jewish ruling council. He came to Jesus at night and said, 'Rabbi, we know that you are a teacher who has come from God. For no one could perform the signs you are doing if God were not with him.'

"Jesus replied, 'Very truly I tell you, no one can see the kingdom of God unless they are born again.'

"'How can someone be born when they are old?' Nicodemus asked. 'Surely they cannot enter a second time into their mother's womb to be born!'

"Jesus answered, 'Very truly I tell you, no one can enter the kingdom of God unless they are born of water and the Spirit. Flesh gives birth to flesh, but the Spirit gives birth to spirit. You should not be surprised at my saying, *You must be born again.* The wind blows wherever it pleases. You hear its sound, but you cannot tell where it comes from or where it is going. So it is with everyone born of the Spirit.'"

Danni lifts her eyes from the passage and looks at me with strength I have never seen on her young face, and I am swept with emotion, deep and abiding. "Father, will you accept Jesus into your heart as your Lord and Savior?"

"I accept that Jesus Christ is almighty God in the flesh."

"And that He was resurrected?"

"As I learned in church many decades ago, Danni, but did not experience at a deep level of understanding, I believe that Jesus died for us and He rose from the dead according to the Scriptures."

"Then let Him take the burdens of your sins off your shoulders, Father. Receive Him into your heart. Will you pray with me?"

"Then let us pray."

We bow our heads in silence and I hear myself speaking tenderly to the Christ, asking for forgiveness of my sins and for His blessings of eternal life. Minutes pass as I feel spiritual enrichment grow with my love for Danni, Kalinda, Jody, and all the women in my life. Helen quietly walks into the room and I glance up; she shakes her head negatively, turns and leaves. Ignoring any intrusion, Danni continues to bow her head in prayer. She squeezes my waist with her arm, sending me a silent message of communion between daughter and father.

I am then aware that on this day of fresh beginnings, my hospice friend Charlie has departed for the great basketball court in the sky. I shall join his team soon enough. But I am still here, his reluctant survivor, a most willing confidant for a fellow athlete, a born-again Christian for my dear Danni.

I have found some painless peace with morphine, although I have never wanted to be one of those who rely on drugs to manage pain. I've pushed through more pain than most mortals, and I've found many ways to reduce pain through meditation and natural endorphins from intense exercise. But exercise is out of the question now, and that which is not used will atrophy. I have been deprived of working out my upper body, so I've have watched my shoulders, biceps, forearms, and pecs shrink to irrelevance. I have been deprived of aerobic fitness and running, so I have seen my quads and calf muscles shrivel to half their former size. I have watched my muscles disintegrate with the passage of time and the success of my final archnemesis, carcinoid cancer.

Yesterday I woke up at five-thirty in the morning, just as the sun was beginning to warm the eastern sky. I walked the hallways of the hospice for twenty-one minutes, feeling liberated by this simple act, which we all take for granted as adults. Movement of any kind helps me feel in control, and you know by now that I have always been a control freak.

Now I understand addiction because morphine numbs my senses and eases the ever-racing cadence of my mind: so much to do; so much that must be left undone. I understand why people get hooked and struggle to be free of addictive substances. And I resist as much as I can, but the pain in my abdomen exceeds the worst stomachache I have ever felt in my life. On a scale of zero to ten, with zero being no pain and ten representing the worst pain you can imagine, then I've been enduring between eight and nine for the previous several days. We continue to aspirate fluid from the eight-inch diameter tumor near my central chest. Yesterday Dr. Sen was good enough to stop by Denver Hospice and remove almost 400cc of brown-yellow liquid, a disgusting demonstration of what this disease can do to the human body. This procedure gave me some time of less pain, even a sense of resurrection for several blessed hours, but the fluids built up again, and now I feel as if I want to scream. The aspirated fluid includes hemoglobin, which means a dramatic drop in my red blood cell count and another reason why I feel so much fatigue. And so, I accept the sweet hypodermic needle with its liquid gift of a heroin derivative. And then I fall into a dream-like state where I am still large and in charge of all my athletic gifts. In those dream states, I am no longer defeated by such a pernicious disease.

I'm somewhat in one of those transcendental states as Jody tiptoes into my room and kisses my head. I reach for her and she snuggles into the bed space next to me. She does not speak for several moments, and I drift in and out of reality, feeling the love she brings to me from times that passed by years ago, losing my sense of here and now, and enjoying a vacation from hospice, as gifted and compassionate as these people of mercy can be.

"Luke, do you know I'm here?" Jody asks with barely a whisper.

"Of course, I do, my sweetheart. Thank you for coming again. I've become a burden for you."

"Don't ever say that. I wish to be here with you every minute but that's not realistic given the current shortage of nurses at the hospital."

"You can be a nurse here?"

"I would love to be a nurse here, but you know they can't pay as well as an intensive care nurse receives. Maybe someday I will."

"What time is it, hon?"

"It's late—after midnight, actually. It has been a very long shift for me today. I started at seven this morning."

"What day is it?"

"Friday."

I weakly shift my body weight, feeling pain surge through my stomach area and chest. For a moment, I have trouble catching my breath, and Jody sits up, a clinical attitude taking charge. "Should I call for the nurse, Luke? She can bring you Roxonol. That will ease your breathlessness."

I know she's suggesting a liquid morphine that is one of their primary tools to fight pain and shortness of breath—near the end of life.

Near the end of life?

She knows something I do not. "Is it really time for Roxonol?" My mouth feels like cotton, without any moisture at all. I reach for a glass and Jody assists me with taking some sips.

"It's up to you, but you're an educated man—my dear man." She softly rests her head on my outstretched arm and curls up again next to me. "I don't want you to fight this, Luke." I can sense that she is crying although she's trying to hide her tears.

"I just want you to be proud of me." Sharp pain hits my chest like a hammer and then quickly subsides. I do not react to this harsh sensation so that she will know and then worry some more.

"I am proud of you beyond the words I have to describe my feelings. You have been a warrior in every sense of the word. During all the years we've been together you have never stopped trying to be the best you can be."

"The enemy is winning." In my mind, I can see the dent in my neck, an ever-present scar that neurogenic sarcoma left me when I was a child, just eight years old.

"You are winning. I know this sounds ridiculous. But you are winning at the only game you have had the option to play." She turns and hugs me like she did the first time we made love together. A sense of hope surges through me, a possibility that I have not felt for a very long time.

"The battle of life?"

"That's it: the battle of life. The inevitable outcome has been wired into our DNA by our Creator, but the path to that outcome is of our choosing. And you have chosen well, Luke."

Tears come to my eyes as I accept her love once again. "I have chosen wellness over illness, strength over weakness, self-empowerment over dependency. I have chosen these things, Jody, and one more."

She lifts her head and considers my eyes, and I can clearly see her piercing blue eyes in the dim light of a midnight room. "What's that, my sweetheart?"

"I have chosen you. I have chosen us. And no cancer, no matter how wicked, can take away that fact of my life. I have always loved you."

She touches my lips with her fingertips and completes my thought. "And I always will."

I am flailing to regain control of my chaotic freefall. Draft from the speeding eighteen-wheeler has blown me out of a practiced and confident vertical trajectory. The Missouri River waits below, not as my liquid lover as I had intended, but as a concrete slab ready to smash my body. I propel my legs as if I'm riding a bicycle, pumping them faster and faster as I descend. Ninety feet. Eighty feet. Seventy feet.

I throw my shoulders back and resist temptation to look down; instead I look ahead, my eyes on the horizon, my focus on the destination. I shift the center of gravity of my body against the downward tug of the earth. I will myself to become a spear, straight, rigid, and piercing—the javelin brandished by a Greek god. Sixty feet. Fifty feet. Forty feet.

I cannot fail for reasons greater than just protecting me from injuries or sudden death but also to prevail over the forces that would defeat me—the forces that can defeat all of us. My enemies are your enemies: illness, disease, weakness, dependency, and withdrawal. So, I am healthy; I am strong; I am independent. And I am connected to life and everyone who shares this mortal plane with me. Thirty feet. Twenty feet. Ten feet.

Approaching sixty-three miles an hour, I am finally in a straight line and certain of my success. Nothing will throw me off this line despite all the complications that have conspired against me. Success is my gift to those who will hear what I must say or read what I must write—all who will learn the lessons I must teach.

Warriors cannot surrender to anything that deters victory. We can never accept complacency. We must not allow setbacks to discourage us from striving and moving forward along the path of our hearts. We will not go quietly into that dark night.

And my toes touch the enrapturing waters of the Missouri. I fall into her depths toward an eternal salvation, a winner.

AFTERWORD

Mark Crooks, PhD, was one of the most influential men in my life. For starters, he liberated me from a self-destructive lifestyle when I was a graduate student at the University of Kansas. Before I met this intense optimist, I had been stumbling dangerously toward a future middle age that could be fraught with illnesses, disabilities, and possibly an early death.

In the context of tumultuous political and cultural upheavals of the early 1970s and under duress from the grind of grad school, I was then smoking one or two packs of cigarettes per day. Marlboros and Winstons were my favorite brands.

My smoking habit found a lot of external reinforcement. A rolling cloud of smoke often poured from the graduate school's departmental offices. Professors smoked, students smoked, Johnny Carson smoked on television, and Steve McQueen smoked on the silver screen. Smoking was a cultural norm for an avant-garde intelligentsia. Nonsmokers seemed to be in a minority, and statistically they almost were, certainly among the male half of the population.

My favored diet involved all the high-fat foods that we know today are bad for us: double cheeseburgers, BLT sandwiches, fried chicken, grilled steaks, bologna and cheddar cheese hoagies. My weekends included imbibing plentiful pitchers of beer or humble bottles of budget wine. I was not inclined to turn down a margarita, an Old Fashioned, or an occasional martini. Heck, I clerked in a liquor store!

Again, this was the early seventies before the nation understood and acknowledged serious health consequences of tobacco, fat-rich diets, and alcohol bingeing among college students, not to mention the overuse of prescription drugs and abuse of psycho-pharmaceutical substances then abundant around college campuses. A popular countercultural mantra back then instructed: *If it feels good, do it.*

So, many of us did—do it.

I embraced some measures of self-restraint, including jogging and eating healthier foods as outlined by the popular nutrition pioneer Adelle Davis, but I had a long journey ahead if I was ever going to modify and discard bad habits adopted in high school and nurtured through my undergraduate years.

Within two weeks after meeting Mark, most of my poor health habits vanished as if I had awakened to a new dawn following a long, self-destructive nightmare. As the years passed, my determination to be physically fit grew almost to the same proportions as that of my mentor.

This book tells a story conveying my impressions of an inimitable man's strong-willed journey toward a healthier, fitter lifestyle, a fitness pioneer who trotted into my life during my college years and remained a continuing presence for almost forty years. Since Mark's teachings and practices were ten- to fifteen years ahead of higher-profile fitness advocates at that time, my account of his life is also a reflection on American society's advancement toward fitness and health awareness.

The lessons that Mark taught me decades ago remain true today as the nation ages. In 2030, one in five American adults will be over age sixty-five, coincidentally the age at which Mark's life concluded. Vital aging and active aging are our mantras today and my departed friend leads the way by his example.

Mark's impact on me was gently compelling from the first day we met at a professor's home in early September 1973 until our concluding in-depth telephone conversations, the lengthiest of which took place on June 14, 2010, for forty-one minutes. That heart-to-heart call ended as most with Mark telling me that he loved my wife, Becky, and me. We loved him back.

I spoke with him one final time on July 5, 2010, when he offered some suggestions about where I might stay near Kansas City Hospice during a trip hurriedly planned. I noticed that he was not enthusiastic about my visit, believing it to be a waste of time. The pragmatic side of Mark also wondered why I would bother taking time to drive so far just to visit with a dying man. He knew that his death was near. One of his friends later informed me that Mark did not want me to see him in such a state of deterioration, knowing that I had always admired his rugged physicality and athletic determination despite all the diseases that had conspired to waste him away. As I rushed to complete some projects and then drive from Denver to Kansas City, Mark passed away, surrounded by his spiritual partner and daughters.

In his final days, Mark struggled with all the malevolent inconveniences of cancer: physical pain, muscle wasting, fatigue, loss, and fear, while nevertheless writing in longhand on a yellow legal pad about his brave journey—an odyssey of an intense man's life.

Mark told me that it was his inclination and plan to include Warrior in the title of his book and write an autobiographical, how-to guide about surviving terminal diseases, especially cancer. In one of our telephone conversations during the last few weeks of his life, he shared with me his last iteration of the book title, *Battles with Cancer: Evolution of a Warrior*. He asked me to help with writing and editing, and I said that I would.

I realized when I began to envision this book—homage to an enigmatic fitness pioneer, daredevil, cancer survivor, and health educator—that I could not capture the truest details of his life, weaving fragments into a typical biography. I recognized the limitations of a fact-based approach: my protagonist had passed away and with him many details about his childhood; military experiences; academic pursuits; and careers in exercise physiology, cardiac rehabilitation, wellness consulting, public speaking, and even home renovation. When Mark died, facts about his life slipped away with him.

Tim O'Brien, the legendary writer and author of *The Things They Carried* and seven other critically acclaimed novels, taught me through his influence about an important distinction between factual truth and emotional truth. The latter is far more important when crafting compelling stories that inculcate universal lessons about life's challenges and triumphs. Therefore, in this book I chose to follow O'Brien's example and instead focused on writing about the emotional, intellectual, and spiritual characteristics of Mark's life—his fortitude as a determined survivor and warrior—while changing supporting characters and circumstances to conform to my cathartic purposes. I also decided to tell the story from Mark's narrative point-of-view, as if he wrote an autobiography during his final days under hospice care.

Although this is a work of fiction—a *biomythography* as Tim O'Brien has labeled the genre—I believe in my heart that I have stayed true to the intensity, integrity, and passions of the late Mark Crooks. I set out to tell a story that would entertain and inspire readers while maintaining accuracy about the essential qualities of a profound human being. To convey this emotional truth, I have fabricated a cast of supporting characters, biographical details, and settings to suit my instincts. Except for the caricature of my protagonist, all other characters and many story settings are fictional and do not represent living persons or accurate depiction of historical events. However, all the daredevil stunts—or feats as Mark preferred to call them—are fact-based, again with modifications in settings and details to suit my narrative. Luke, the fictional lead character, is as daring as the man who inspired the character.

Mark never gave up on his survival until one fateful day in early May 2010. He asked me for help, and I agreed to drive him to St. Louis where he would be evaluated by a team of physicians as to his suitability for a liver transplant. Not long before departing to meet with transplant specialists, Mark's attending oncologist informed him that he would never be approved for a new liver, the only remaining option. According to his physician, prospective organ transplant patients must be free of cancer for at least five years. Mark had beaten prostate cancer just weeks before liver tumors became evident. He understood then—but perhaps did not quite accept at first—that this medical prognosis, while accurate, was a death sentence; his knowledge of human physiology and anatomy assured unambiguous clarity about an inescapable destiny.

For the next several weeks before his death, I struggled with awareness that Mark's attending oncologist was not being completely forthright about his medical situation and treatment options. The oncologist continued to care for Mark with "technological medicine" rather than another, more peaceful alternative: palliative care, also known as hospice.

I have been a keynote speaker several times at national and state conferences for executives in the hospice industry, and I have been a caretaker for my own parents and sister, who also received hospice care. I have learned that hospice provides painkilling and soothing care for those who have terminal medical conditions. The medical focus is comfort not curative. Hospice can be found in freestanding, often home-like facilities, within patient homes, or in hospitals and nursing homes. Services include pain control, nursing care, spiritual counsel, and many other nurturing services.

A major goal of hospice is to help patients experience maximum possible peace and comfort during the final months, weeks, or days. Life-prolonging medical intervention has its value when the outcome allows greater life quality if not extension of time remaining, but when medical procedures promote more pain and illness without recovery, it is time to put the brakes on "heroic medicine." Hospice also provides bereavement counseling and support groups for family members of those who are dying or have passed away.

I believed then, as I do today, that Mark had reached the endpoint of his need for further diagnostic tests, experimental procedures, esoteric chemotherapies, or pharmaceutical interventions—other than pain management and some help with gastrointestinal issues that are an uncomfortable consequence of liver disease. My hero did not require further heroic intrusions by modern medicine. He needed and wanted as many peaceful, pain-free days as possible so that he could complete writing his book, conclude his relationships with those he loved, and seek spiritual guidance and support. He needed liberation from hope after fifty-seven years of not allowing cancer to get in the way of hope. He told me plainly that he was tired of needles, procedures, and pain.

Following my insistent counseling, Mark asked his oncologist several precise questions about the status of his cancer and prognosis. Direct questions engendered direct answers. He learned that he would die soon because of liver failure. His acceptance immediately followed, thank goodness.

Also because of my frustration and irritation with the traditional medical focus on curative intervention, I called Bev Sloan, then CEO of The Denver Hospice. I explained Mark's situation to Bev, and she referred me to her counterpart at the Kansas City Hospice, propitiously located near Mark's residence. With encouragement and gentle nudging, Mark met with a hospice representative and learned about available services.

Hospice care began at home, but for the final few days he moved to the Kansas City Hospice House, located just blocks from his home. Hospice care relieved him of most of the torment until his final breath on July 8, 2010.

Unfortunately, hospice could only provide respite care during the last few days rather than weeks or months. This is all too typical: patients and their families wait too long to explore the full range of benefits and services available through hospice. They fail to explore the hospice alternative near the beginning of the dying process and wait instead until the end. In many cases, earlier intervention can mitigate much suffering and afford dying patients' extra quality time to finish their business before passing away peacefully—to have a "good death" as each terminally ill person defines it.

Mark's story has vast implications for his peers—the tens of millions of Silent Generation members and Baby Boomers who have aged beyond fifty and are peering into a future where vitality and even survival will require toughness, wellness knowledge, and commitment—a Warrior's comportment. Mark believed that his second and final book could also provide a wellness toolkit to help aging adults survive and thrive during their concluding years. His larger mission had been to teach all of us what it takes to survive cancer for fifty-seven years and do well no matter what happens, up to and including our final days.

As his friend, I have done my best to carry his mission and lessons forward.

Brent Green

BRENT GREEN

A sthma almost killed Brent at age four; cancer almost killed Mark at age eight. Their chance encounter during college changed Brent's life, dedicating him to sharing Mark's story, including this biomythography novel. WARRIOR continues Brent's twenty-year journey to help change what it means to grow old, as well as to advance society's conceptions of chronic diseases and dying with dignity. Brent is a media communications strategist, creative director, writer, speaker, trainer, and consultant focusing on generational marketing. He is author of two business books: *Marketing to Leading-Edge Baby Boomers* and *Generation Reinvention*. His most recent nonfiction book is *Questions of the Spirit: The Quest for Understanding at A Time of Loss*. His fiction titles include *Noble Chaos: A Novel* and *Are You Still Listening?* He writes for online and traditional print media, and he analyzes current affairs through his blog

BRENT GREEN

Boomers: A Trip into the Heart of the Baby Boomer Generation. An honors graduate of the University of Kansas with a BA in psychology and communications, he completed master's studies in counseling psychology.

www.ingramcontent.com/pod-product-compliance
Lightning Source LLC
Chambersburg PA
CBHW022113040426
42450CB00006B/688